Documenting Southern Ethiopia

Recognizing past legacies and forging the way forward

FROBENIUS-INSTITUT
FÜR KULTURANTHROPOLOGISCHE FORSCHUNG
AN DER GOETHE-UNIVERSITÄT FRANKFURT

Joint publication by the Frobenius-Institut, Frankfurt am Main, and Mekelle University

in cooperation with Hawassa University

Extra issue of ITYOP̣IS (NEAJ), volume 3 (2017)

ITYOP̣IS (NEAJ) appears annually. In addition, special issues are published on an irregular basis. This extra issue has been produced in cooperation with the Frobenius-Institut in Frankfurt/Main as a joint publication in cooperation with Hawassa University.

This special issue came out of the conference 'Documenting Southern Ethiopia: Recognizing Past Legacies and Forging the Way Forward' organized by Hawassa University in cooperation with the Frobenius Institute in February 2017, and was supported by a DFG grant.

Guest Editors of the Extra Issue:
Elias Alemu (Hawassa University) – Sophia Thubauville (Frobenius-Institut)

Series editor of the ITYOP̣IS (NEAJ) Extra Issues:
Wolbert G. C. Smidt (2017)

Language Editor: Kay Celtel
Webpage Administrator: Steffen Kirchner, Wolbert G. C. Smidt

Cover photos: Front: Tiya stelae, © Frobenius-Institut (Sign. PBA-B 00341);
Back: Inset plantation, Kambaataa, November 2005, © Wolbert G.C. Smidt
Cover design: Gebremichael Nguse, Mekelle
Layout: Thomas Rave, Hamburg

Distribution outside Northeastern Africa: Frobenius-Institut, Frankfurt am Main; LIT Verlag, Münster

ISSN 2223-7178 (Mekelle University)
ISBN 978-3-643-91040-0 (pb)
ISBN 978-3-643-96040-5 (PDF)

ITYOP̣IS

Mekelle University, Tigray, Ethiopia
Editorial office: College of Social Sciences and Languages (CSSL)
Email: Ityopis.MU@gmail.com | Internet: www.ityopis.org
P.O. Box 2239, Mekelle, Tigray | Electronic version: AJOL.org
Ethiopia

ITYOP̣IS

ኢትዮጲስ

Northeast African Journal
of Social Sciences and Humanities

Extra Issue, Volume 3

2018

Documenting Southern Ethiopia

Recognizing past legacies and forging the way forward

Proceedings of the Workshop at Hawassa University

edited by
Sophia Thubauville and Elias Alemu

2018
Münster: LIT Verlag – Mekelle: Mekelle University

Bibliographic information published by the Deutsche Nationalbibliothek
The Deutsche Nationalbibliothek lists this publication in the Deutsche Nationalbibliografie; detailed bibliographic data are available on the Internet at http://dnb.d-nb.de.

ISBN 978-3-643-91040-0 (pb)
ISBN 978-3-643-96040-5 (PDF)

Distribution:
In the UK: Global Book Marketing, e-mail: mo@centralbooks.com
In North America: Independent Publishers Group, e-mail: orders@ipgbook.com
In Germany: LIT Verlag Fresnostr. 2, D-48159 Münster
Tel. +49 (0) 2 51-620 32 22, Fax +49 (0) 2 51-922 60 99, e-mail: vertrieb@lit-verlag.de
e-books are available at www.litwebshop.de

Table of Contents

Introduction

ELIAS ALEMU and SOPHIA THUBAUVILLE

The contributions to this special issue came out of the 'Documenting Southern Ethiopia: Recognizing Past Legacies and Forging the Way Forward' conference organized by Hawassa University in cooperation with the Frobenius Institute, Frankfurt in February 2017. The idea of bringing together international scholars for the conference came up in the course of a research project aimed at indexing and digitizing the archival material on Ethiopian Studies at the Frobenius Institute. The project, entitled 'Indexing and Digitizing of the Archival Material on Ethiopian Studies of the Frobenius Institute', was funded by the German Research Foundation and ran from September 2014 to August 2017. The comprehensive visual documentation of southern Ethiopia between 1934 and 1974 was extraordinary and nearly all the ethnographic research explored in that project was pioneering work, since not much research had been done in southern Ethiopia before the 1930s. Apart from indexing and digitizing the archival material, which dates back to the very first research activities undertaken by the Frobenius Institute on southern Ethiopia, the project intended to open up a dialogue about the research activities, research findings and methodological approaches of former institute members. The first part of this dialogue was a lecture series in which internationally renowned scholars commented on the research of the Frobenius Institute members in southern Ethiopia. The second part was a series of reviews from Ethiopian anthropologists who spent time in the archives of the institute. These critical assessments were then brought together and published in 2017 (Dinslage and Thubauville 2017).

The conference at Hawassa University was devised as the third part of this dialogue. Instead of merely focusing on the earlier research activities of the Frobenius Institute, the conference was meant to show that the research findings of the past are still relevant in today's ethnography of southern Ethiopia. Given the pioneering studies carried out by researchers affiliated to the Frobenius Institute and the growing achievements of Hawassa University in problem-solving research and technology transfer, the conference was specifically designed to create a platform for discussion and exchange of ideas by mapping out key trends over the last eight decades in southern Ethiopia.

With the exception of Hanna, all the articles in this special issue were presented at the conference at Hawassa University.

The first two articles (Thubauville and Getachew) mainly focus on the research done by members of the Frobenius Institute in southern Ethiopia. While Thubauville gives an overview of the research activities, publications and archival material that can be found today in Frankfurt, Getachew's contribution on the age grade system of the Gedeo provides one example of the relevance and insights that can be gained from unpublished work found in the archives of the Frobenius Institute, in this case, an ethnography by A.E. Jensen on the Gedeo.

Epple and Gellebo, the authors of the next two articles, also tackle the published and unpublished material of the Frobenius researchers (compare also their earlier publications Epple 2017, Kansite 2017). Their contributions in this issue focus on two topics that were of central interest to the Frobenius researchers: the crafts people and slaves (Epple) and ancestral statues (*waakka*) of the Konso (Kansite). Both issues are of renewed relevance today: social categories because of ethnic federalism, which has led to a revival of cultural values and local traditions; and *waakka* because of increased tourism and the global art market's interest in these sculptures.

The remaining five contributions focus on current research. Conducted by Ethiopian researchers currently working in different Higher Education Institutions within Ethiopia, these contributions can be grouped under three broad themes: women and gender studies; conflicts and frontiers; and indigenous religions and biodiversity. The topics being researched show that anthropology training and research in Ethiopia is rooted in practical application, partly because researchers have an obligation to do community work (see Bosha and Temechegn), and partly because research in Ethiopia is often commissioned by governmental and non-governmental organizations (Zerihun). The contributions of Ethiopian researchers have played an important role during the above mentioned conference not only in bringing scholars working in southern Ethiopia together but also in creating a much-needed platform for debate among researchers and other stakeholders who are interested in the various issues raised.

Two contributions – Hanna's work on the Maale of southern Ethiopia and Temechegn and Bosha's work on the Alle of southern Ethiopia – fall into the category of women and gender studies. While Hanna explores the active role women take in devising survival strategies among the Maale people in the face of prolonged contact and interaction with outsiders; Temechegn and Bosha turn our attention to the practice of marriage among the Alle, shedding light on polygamy, the status of women in it and the changes observed in its practice through time.

Elias's work on the Nyangatom of southwestern Ethiopia and Nigussie's contribution on the Gedeo of southern Ethiopia fall into the second category: conflicts and frontiers. Elias focuses on the myriad of intertwined scenarios that shape the voices, experiences and lives of the Nyangatom along the borderlands adjoining Ethiopia, Kenya and South Sudan. Nigussie explores the process of conflict resolution from the perspective of the Gedeo, showing us that the breakdown of communication might lead to conflict, and that folk media can provide the means by which it is resolved.

Last but not least, Zerihun's contribution focuses on the linked endangerment of indigenous religions, ecology and biodiversity in southern Ethiopia. He argues that, as most native religions are seriously endangered today, syncretism may be an important factor in the continuity of at least certain elements of these religions and their positive effects on biodiversity.

References

DINSLAGE, Sabine and Sophia THUBAUVILLE

2017 *Seeking Out Wise Old Men. Six Decades of Ethiopian Studies at the Frobenius Institute Revisited.* Berlin: Reimer.

EPPLE, Susanne

2017 'Definite segregation or permeable boundaries? Revisiting the Frobenius research on artisans, hunters and slave descendants in Ethiopia', in: Sabine DINSLAGE und Sophia THUBAUVILLE (eds.), *Seeking Out Wise Old Men. Six Decades of Ethiopian Studies at the Frobenius Institute Revisited*, 90–108. Berlin: Reimer.

KANSITE GELLEBO

2017 'Social divisions and their gradual transformation among the Konso in southern Ethiopia', in: Sabine DINSLAGE und Sophia THUBAUVILLE (eds.), *Seeking Out Wise Old Men. Six Decades of Ethiopian Studies at the Frobenius Institute Revisited*, 109–123. Berlin: Reimer.

Six Decades of Southern Ethiopian Studies at the Frobenius Institute

SOPHIA THUBAUVILLE

The Beginnings – Captivated by Southern Ethiopia

The regional focus and interest of the Frobenius Institute on southern Ethiopia was in some ways already initiated by its founder Leo Frobenius, although he died in 1938 without ever travelling to Ethiopia himself. Frobenius was a well-known expert on Africa and founded the institute 1898 on basis of his private collection under the name "Afrika Archiv". Frobenius was well-connected and amongst others also a friend of Emperor Wilhelm II. His contact to the emperor and nationalist attitude made him to travel to Northeast Africa in 1914 with plans to initiate a revolt against the British in Sudan (Braukämper 1994, Thubauville 2014). He went by the Red Sea and was meant to reach Sudan via Ethiopia, but was uncovered by the Italians in Eritrea and sent back to Europe. Before returning to Europe, he was able to shortly visit Eritrea's Hamasen region. There he took photographs and drew few sketches of rock engravings that he observed.[1] Unfortunately, this short stay and impression of Eritrea remained his only visit to Northeast Africa. Still, Frobenius kept an interest in the region. In the 1920s the Austrian researcher Friedrich Julius Bieber – who had already made a name for himself as a leading scholar on Ethiopia with his ethnography of the Kaffa – became a corresponding member of the institute. Together with Frobenius he published the volume "Zur Herrlichkeit des Sudans" (Concerning the Glory of Sudan), the edited travel report of a fellow Austrian, Eduard Freiherr von Gallot, who had travelled through Ethiopia in 1831. The two scholars had planned common research expeditions to Northeast Africa together, but unfortunately Bieber died in 1924.

In 1932 Frobenius was appointed Honorary Professor at Frankfurt University and shortly after was additionally engaged as director of the ethnographic museum. Frobenius was therefore, busy with his tasks in Frankfurt. The institute's focus covered not only ethnography but also prehistory. This is why the researchers were heavily inspired by descriptions of the French archaeologists Azaïs and Chambard of the large number of monoliths to be found in southern Ethiopia (Azaïs and Chambard 1931). Frobenius decided on an expedition to Ethiopia and hand over the directorship of it to Jensen, one of his assistants. Jensen had won Frobenius' trust in the course of two expeditions to South Africa and Libya. He left Frankfurt for Ethiopia in October 1934, accompanied by fellow researchers and a painter. Stirred by the French researchers' discovery of prehistoric stele, they seemed to have been preoccupied with the thought of similar discoveries. They travelled south along the lakes of the Rift Valley and on a small hill, Tutto Fela, in the Gedeo area, they finally found what they were searching for, around one hundred phallus-shaped stone steles with incised faces and geometrical patterns (Thubauville 2012 a and b).

1 Rock art was one of the main research interests of Frobenius (Kuba 2017).

Fig 1: Stone stela at Tutto Fela, 1935

The southernmost point they reached was Konso. There, Jensen did pioneering research on the *gada* system and *waka* (wooden memorial steles). Within a year after their return to Frankfurt in 1935, Jensen had already managed to publish their findings in the voluminous monograph "Im Landes des Gada" (In the Land of Gada). He had caught fire with research in Ethiopia and especially the Konso region. However, the political situation short before World War II did not permit him to return soon. All the male researchers at the Frobenius Institute were finally recruited as soldiers. The female members of the institute tried to keep some activities going and rescue the institute and its collections during this difficult period.[2] One of the women was Elisabeth Pauli, a trained painter who had joined the institute in 1933 and participated in several expeditions under the lead of Frobenius. During the years at the institute, Pauli became interested in ethnography herself. She and another female institute member, Agnes Schulz, spent the war preparing literature reviews on the peoples of southern Ethiopia. Though after the war men took over leading roles in the expeditions and research again, it is the work and publications of these two women that lay the foundations for the institute's post-war expeditions to Ethiopia (Pauli 1944, 1950; Schulz 1941/43).

2 The women hid the collections of the institute in different non-private and private houses in Frankfurt and its surrounding. Unfortunately, some of them were hit by bombs in March 1944. Therefore, parts of the pre-WW2 collection of the institute and also all notebooks and diaries of the first expedition to Ethiopia, are lost.

Under the Goodwill of the Emperor

After World War II ended, Jensen returned from the front. In 1946 he became the new director of the institute. Together with Pauli – who would eventually become his wife – he soon began to prepare the next expedition to south Ethiopia. In 1950 two young research assistants, Eike Haberland and Willy Schulz-Weidner, joined the institute and the expedition team. Both of them had just earned their PhDs in Social Anthropology, Haberland under the supervision of Jensen and Schulz-Weidner from the University of Mainz. The four team members left Frankfurt for Ethiopia in September 1950 and were the first German social anthropologists to go on expedition after World War II. They planned to travel as far south as Chew Bahir and the Dassanach people, but logistical problems, especially the shortage and fast exhaustion of mules, prevented them from reaching further south than the Hamar Mountains. Once they had reached the south of the country, the research team split up to study as many ethnic groups as possible. Therefore, they mostly spent only a few weeks in one place. The research aimed at doing short surveys of a then still terra incognita instead of doing a thematically deep study of one group. While the other team members already went back to Frankfurt in autumn 1951, Haberland continued his research among the Borana until summer 1952.

Fig 2: Exhausted mules limited the study area

The next expedition to Ethiopia took place in 1954. The core of the team, Jensen and Pauli – now a married couple – and Haberland, remained the same. They were joined by two young researchers, one of them Helmut Straube, who later became professor in Munich. In his trip, Haberland wanted to clarify some data he had collected among the Borana and spent several weeks among the Wolayta, Jensen and Pauli did their main research among the Sidama, and Straube concentrated on the ethnography of the Western

Cushitic people.[3] The major outcomes of these two expeditions in the 1950s were three large ethnographies, all of which shared a similar style and structure while dealing with different peoples: Jensen's *Altvölker Süd-Äthiopiens* (1959), Straube's *Westkuschitische Völker Süd-Äthiopiens* (1963), and Haberland's *Galla Süd-Äthiopiens* (1963). Like a major survey, they provided, above all, a short overview of the social organization, religious life, life cycle, material culture, and oral history of the studied peoples. The appendices of the ethnographies contained drawings of material culture as well as a good number of photographs. In addition to the broad ethnographies, Haberland used his collected data, especially the one from Wolayta, for his habilitation thesis on Ethiopian kingdoms (Haberland 1965). In 1967 he returned to Wolayta, where he studied the history and political organization more in depth. The findings from this second visit to Wolayta remain unpublished until today (see Abbink 2006; Barata 2017).

Material for three more ethnographies – a second one on the Konso (see Kansite 2017), one on Sidama (see Ambaye 2017), and one on Gedeo (see Getachew this volume and 2017) – was also collected by Jensen, but for different reasons the ethnographies remained unpublished. The main cause was Jensen's bad health condition after his return from the last Ethiopia expedition. He died in 1965, shortly after his retirement.

Fig 3: The team of the 1950/51 expedition in their camp in Maale

Haberland became the new director of the Frobenius Institute in 1968. Apart from a short sojourn to Oceania, he continued the focus on Ethiopian Studies at the Institute and initiated three more research expeditions to southern Ethiopia. In 1970–1971 Haberland went again to southern Ethiopia, this time to study the history of the Had-

3 Straube called the Cushitic language speakers located west of the Rift Valley lakes as "West Cushitic peoples".

iya, Dauro and Gofa. He was accompanied by three institute members, among them Ulrich Braukämper, who later became professor at Göttingen. During his final expedition to Ethiopia from 1972 to 1974 Haberland, Braukämper and the doctoral student Werner Lange, conducted studies among the Hadiya, Sidama, Oromo, Gamo, Gofa, Kefa and Dizi.

While the earlier expeditions of the 1930s and 1950s had been organized as group undertakings, from the 1960s onwards – even if several people travelled together – the research projects were more individual and driven by specific research interests. This was due, on the one hand, to changing discourses in social anthropology, but on the other hand, to changes in the financing of research trips. Beginning in the 1960s, research trips to Ethiopia were mainly funded by travel funds for individual research projects, whereas before a complex system of fundraising (see Dinslage 2017) had been applied to finance expedition trips.

The comprehensive, survey-like ethnographies, which resulted from the expeditions of the 1950s were often criticized for their lack and/or obsolete theoretical contribution as well as a lack of timely methodology (see Abbink 2017; Fleming and Lewis 1961). The research interests of Frobenius Institute members involved in Ethiopian Studies at that time were above all cultural history (Abbink 2017; Bustorf 2014), prehistory (Kuba 2017; Thubauville 2012a and 2012b), the meritorious complex (Braukämper 2014), social stratification (see Epple 2017 and Kansite 2017), and the history of south Ethiopian kingships (see Data 2017).

Continuous contact with Emperor Haile Selassie had smoothed the way for the research activities of Jensen, Haberland and the other institute members. They regularly met the ruler after arriving in Ethiopia and his letters of recommendation guaranteed them the constant help of the administration and police forces in the south of the coun-

Fig 4: Jensen with the emperor in 1950

try.[4] Haile Selassie also personally allowed the researchers to transport items of cultural heritage like the above mentioned stone stele to Germany (Thubauville 2012b: 86–88). The most obvious sign of the close relationship between Haile Selassie and the researchers was the fact that Haberland was awarded of the Haile Selassie Prize for Ethiopian Studies in 1971.

Research during the Derg Regime

After Haile Selassie's overthrow and the advent of the socialist regime in 1974, the research trips by the Frobenius Institute in Ethiopia came to an end. Haberland shifted his area of active research to West Africa, but he still had a lot of unpublished material from his former research trips and his publications on Ethiopia after 1974 were as numerous as those from his years of active study. Especially his last book – on social stratification among the Dizi – kept him busy until the very end of his career and finally had to be published posthumously (Haberland 1993).

During the socialist regime Haberland further kept an active interest in Ethiopia by supervising two Ethiopian PhD students in Frankfurt. The first student, Asfa-Wossen Asserate, a grand-nephew of Haile Selassie, was already enrolled as Haberland's PhD student when his father was executed during the socialist revolution. After earning his PhD,[5] he stayed in Germany and became a well-known writer. Through his books,[6] he greatly influences the German image of, and knowledge about, Ethiopia. Negasso Gidada, Haberland's second PhD student, came to Germany in 1974. While studying for his PhD,[7] he held different offices within European Oromo associations and the Oromo Liberation Front in Europe. He returned to Ethiopia directly after the fall of the socialist regime and went on to become Ethiopia's first democratically elected president.

The second institute member who continued to be very active in Ethiopian Studies during the socialist regime was Ulrich Braukämper. Although he was unable to carry out research inside Ethiopia in that period, he became actively involved in assisting Ethiopian refugees in Germany and Ethiopia's neighbouring countries like Sudan and Somalia. With the death of Haberland in 1992 and Braukämper's move to Göttingen, where he became professor in 1994, the Frobenius Institute's focus on Ethiopian Studies temporarily came to an end.

4 Policemen and other administrative personnel of the imperial regime were essential for the work of the expedition members as they supplied them with accommodation, helped in locating food supplies and pack animals and were often the only people who could translate local languages to Amharic or English. The use of administrators and policemen as intermediators, of course, was at the same time a limitation, especially when it came to translations.

5 He earned his PhD in 1978 for the thesis "Die Geschichte von Sawa (Äthiopien) 1700–1865. Nach dem Tarika nagast des Belatten Geta Heruy Walda Sellase" (The history of Sawa (Ethiopia) 1700–1865. After the Tarika nagast by Belatten Geta Heruy Walda Sellase).

6 Most of his books are concerned with German culture and manners, questions of migration and integration and his family history. His book "Manieren" (manners) became a bestseller and he already received several German awards for his books as well as the federal cross of merit.

7 He earned his PhD in 1984 for his thesis „History of the Sayyoo Oromoo of Southwestern Wallaga, Ethiopia, from about 1730 to 1886".

Legacies of Six Decades

Sixty years of research involving eleven researchers have left a big imprint in the archives of the Frobenius Institute. The scientific legacies of Jensen and Haberland stored in the institute's archive include various written documents, such as diaries and notebooks, travel reports, letters from, within and to the field, scripts for lectures, hand-drawn maps and even four unpublished manuscripts of ethnographies. The institute also has an administrative archive, which provides an insight into the financing of the expeditions to Ethiopia (Dinslage 2017). As the Frobenius Institute continuously put a great deal of effort into the visual documentation and collection of material culture, today more than 20,000 photographs and sketches, 83 film reels (Thubauville 2017) and around 1,200 ethnographic objects (Glück 2017) from the expeditions to southern Ethiopia can be found in the institute's various archives.

Between 2014 and 2017 the "Indexing and Digitizing of the Archival Material on Ethiopian Studies of the Frobenius Institute" project, financed by the German Research Foundation, has been indexing and sustainably archiving all of the above-mentioned material concerning Ethiopian Studies from the legacies of the Frobenius Institute. The project facilitated public access to these documents through an open-access database.[8]

Fig 5: Shelf with objects from Ethiopia in the ethnographic collection

As some of the methodological and theoretical parameters under which the researchers worked back then are obsolete and controversial today, the digitizing and indexing of the data was accompanied by a critical discussion of it. Furthermore, the dialogue with Ethiopian colleagues had been a central element of the project. Several colleagues had been invited to Frankfurt to deal with the archival material and review it from an Ethiopian perspective. Three of them – Ambaye Ogato, Getachew Senishaw and Kansite Gellebo – present their findings in this

8 www.frobenius-institut.de/aethiopien-datenbank

volume.[9] The project furthermore financed a lecture series with leading international researchers such as Herbert Lewis, Jon Abbink, Ulrich Braukämper and Ivo Strecker. Their presentations discussed important methodological and theoretical problems around the contributions of Frobenius Institute researchers to the study of southern Ethiopia.[10]

The indexing, digitizing and reviews of the archival material were just a first step in the engagement with the archival material on Ethiopia at the Frobenius Institute. Although the published as well as the unpublished material has, as above mentioned, theoretical as well as methodological shortcomings – especially seen from today's perspective – the only adequate way to deal with the material is to translate it into English and by that way make it available to the increasing number of Ethiopian scholars for whom the material is an important contribution to their country's cultural diversity and history.

References

ABBINK, Jon

2006 Reconstructing Haberland Reconstructing the Wolaitta: Writing the History and Society of a Former Ethiopian Kingdom. *History in Africa* 33: 1–15.

2017 'Wie es eigentlich gewesen …': Eike Haberland's Rankean approach to southern Ethiopian cultures and its legacy today,' in: Sabine DINSLAGE und Sophia THUBAUVILLE (eds.), *Seeking out wise old men. Six decades of Ethiopian Studies at the Frobenius Institute revisited*, 155–175. Berlin: Reimer.

AMBAYE OGATO

2017 'A cursory reflection on the research of the Frobenius Institute on the Sidama people of Ethiopia', in: Sabine DINSLAGE und Sophia THUBAUVILLE (eds.), *Seeking out wise old men. Six decades of Ethiopian Studies at the Frobenius Institute revisited*, 251–264. Berlin: Reimer.

AZAÏS, François B. and Roger CHAMBARD

1931 *Cinq années de recherches archéologiques en Ethiopie*. Paris: Geuthner.

BARATA, Data Dea

2017 'Goldmine and Minefield. A Native Anthropologist's Review of E. Haberland's Culture-Historical Research on Wolaita, Ethiopia', in: Sabine DINSLAGE und Sophia THUBAUVILLE (eds.), *Seeking out wise old men. Six decades of Ethiopian Studies at the Frobenius Institute revisited*, 237–249. Berlin: Reimer.

BRAUKÄMPER, Ulrich

1994 'Frobenius as political agent: Journey to Eritrea in 1915', in: Harold G. MARCUS (ed.), *New trends in Ethiopian Studies. Papers of the 12th International Conference of Ethiopian Studies*, 553–561. Lawrenceville: Africa World Press.

9 Their findings, as well as an article by another colleague of Ethiopian origin, Data Dea Barata, can further be read in the publication "Seeking out wise old men. Six decades of Ethiopian Studies at the Frobenius Institute revisited" (Dinslage and Thubauville 2017).

10 Most of their presentations were published in the above mentioned publication.

2014 'The meritorious complex. A research focus of the Frobenius Institute in Ethiopia', in: Wolbert SMIDT and Sophia THUBAUVILLE (eds.), *Cultural research in northeast Africa. German histories and stories*, 205–211. Frankfurt, Mekelle: Frobenius-Institut.

BUSTORF, Dirk

2014 'Adolf Ellegard Jensen, Eike Haberland and the Frankfurt research tradition in southern Ethiopia', in: Wolbert SMIDT and Sophia THUBAUVILLE (eds.), *Cultural research in northeast Africa. German histories and stories*, 185–195. Frankfurt, Mekelle: Frobenius-Institut.

DINSLAGE, Sabine

2017 'How to finance an expedition? Insights from the archives of the Frobenius Institute', in: Sabine DINSLAGE und Sophia THUBAUVILLE (eds.), *Seeking out wise old men. Six decades of Ethiopian Studies at the Frobenius Institute revisited*, 179–201. Berlin: Reimer.

DINSLAGE, Sabine and Sophia THUBAUVILLE

2017 *Seeking out wise old men. Six decades of Ethiopian Studies at the Frobenius Institute revisited.* Berlin: Reimer.

EPPLE, Susanne

2017 'Definite segregation or permeable boundaries? Revisiting the Frobenius research on artisans, hunters and slave descendants in Ethiopia,' in: Sabine DINSLAGE und Sophia THUBAUVILLE (eds.), *Seeking out wise old men. Six decades of Ethiopian Studies at the Frobenius Institute revisited*, 90–108. Berlin: Reimer.

FLEMING, Harold C. and Herbert S. LEWIS

1961 Review of Altvölker Süd-Äthiopiens by Ad. E. Jensen. *American Anthropologist* 63(3): 615–616.

FROBENIUS, Leo and Friedrich Julius BIEBER (eds.)

1923 *Zur Herrlichkeit des Sudans.* Stuttgart, Berlin, Leipzig: Deutsche Verlagsgesellschaft.

GETACHEW Senishaw

2017 'The Gedeo. Jensen's ethnographic perspective', in: Sabine DINSLAGE und Sophia THUBAUVILLE (eds.), *Seeking out wise old men. Six decades of Ethiopian Studies at the Frobenius Institute revisited*, 265–280. Berlin: Reimer.

GLÜCK, Kim

2017 'Collection activities of the Frobenius Institute. Expeditions to southern Ethiopia', in: Sabine DINSLAGE und Sophia THUBAUVILLE (eds.), *Seeking out wise old men. Six decades of Ethiopian Studies at the Frobenius Institute revisited*, 203–220. Berlin: Reimer.

HABERLAND, Eike Friedrich Georg

1963 *Galla Süd-Äthiopiens. Ergebnisse der Frobenius-Expeditionen 1950–52 und 1954–56*. Stuttgart: Kohlhammer.

1965 *Untersuchungen zum Äthiopischen Königtum*. Wiesbaden: Franz Steiner Verlag.

1993 *Hierarchie und Kaste. Zur Geschichte und Politischen Struktur der Dizi in Südwest-Äthiopien*. Stuttgart: Franz Steiner Verlag.

JENSEN, Adolf Ellegard

1936 *Im Lande des Gada. Wanderungen zwischen Volkstrümmern Südabessiniens*. Strecker und Schröder: Stuttgart.

1959 *Altvölker Süd-Äthiopiens*. Stuttgart: Kohlhammer.

KANSITE Gellebo

2017 'Social divisions and their gradual transformation among the Konso in southern Ethiopia', in: Sabine DINSLAGE und Sophia THUBAUVILLE (eds.), *Seeking out wise old men. Six decades of Ethiopian Studies at the Frobenius Institute revisited*, 109–123. Berlin: Reimer.

KUBA, Richard

2017 'The Frobenius Institute's study of rock art in Ethiopia', in: Sabine DINSLAGE und Sophia THUBAUVILLE (eds.), *Seeking out wise old men. Six decades of Ethiopian Studies at the Frobenius Institute revisited*, 125–135. Berlin: Reimer.

PAULI, Elisabeth

1944 Die Stämme Nördlich des Rudolfsees. *Beiträge zur Kolonialforschung* 6:73–79.

1950 Die Splitterstämme Nördlich des Rudolfsees: Studie über wenig bekannte Völker Ost-Afrikas. *Annali Lateranensi* 14:61–191.

SCHULZ, Agnes

1941/43 Sidama-Völker in Abessinien. *Paideuma* 2:140–146.

STRAUBE, Helmut

1963 *Westkuschitische Völker Süd-Äthiopiens*. Stuttgart: Kohlhammer.

THUBAUVILLE, Sophia

2012a 'Schlummernde Heiligtümer', in: Clementine DELISS (ed.), *Objekt Atlas - Feldforschung im Museum*, 375–385. Bielefeld: Kerber.

2012b Memorial for heroes. *Tribal Art* 64:84–91.

2014 'Leo Frobenius and northeast Africa: An indiscreet secret mission and the foundation of Ethiopian Studies at the Frobenius Institute', in: Wolbert SMIDT and Sophia THUBAUVILLE (eds.), *Cultural research in northeast Africa. German histories and stories*, 173–183. Frankfurt am Main, Mekelle: Frobenius-Institut.

2017 'Involuntary pioneers of ethnographic film in southern Ethiopia', in: Sabine DINSLAGE and Sophia THUBAUVILLE (eds.), *Seeking out wise old men. Six decades of Ethiopian Studies at the Frobenius Institute revisited*, 221–235. Berlin: Reimer.

List of illustrations

The Gedeo after Jensen's Ethnografic Fieldwork[1]

Changes and Continuities in Religion and the *Baalle* System

GETACHEW SENISHAW

Introduction

Jensen, together with his colleagues from the Frobenius Institute, made two field trips to the land of the Gedeo: the first took place in 1934/5[2] and the second in 1955. In his unpublished manuscript detailing the trip, he noted that the objective of the second field visit was to understand if and how socio-economic dynamics had changed since 1935 (Getachew 2017).[3] Jensen's 1955 manuscript serves as a starting point from which to trace and understand changes and continuities among the Gedeo since 1955. During the two periods of fieldwork, the German research team took more than 500 black-and-white photographs and produced documentary films[4] on ensete (*Ensete Ventricosum*) plantation and processing, tanning, and mourning ceremonies. The photos show different aspects of Gedeo daily life, such as dressing styles, marketplaces, landscapes, mourning and *baalle* – the Gedeo political and grade system – grade ceremonies. These are important documents for understanding developments among the Gedeo, since there is no other photographic documentation from that time. My own fieldwork among the Gedeo was conducted in 2012/13 and 2016 in Mekonesa Kebele, and explored Gedeo *baalle*, religion and other ethnographic issues. I used a qualitative approach to explore, describe and interpret major issues that required in-depth analysis. Participant observation was employed to observe everyday events and rituals. Unstructured and semi-structured interviews were held with interviewees drawn from diverse sections of the society. In order to generate data from different groups, focus group discussions were held with men, women and youths.

Following this introduction are four sections: the first section describes the study area; the second discusses Gedeo religion and spiritual life; the third is about the Gedeo *baalle*

1 My special thanks go to the Frobenius Institute at Frankfurt University for financing my trip to Germany to access the archival materials on which this article is based.

2 The findings of the first research trip are published in Jensen 1936, the travel report in Jensen 1936 as well as in Wohlenberg 1988.

3 The manuscripts and documents of the legacies of Jensen and Haberland are being digitalized, analysed and made available to the public through the, 'Indexing and Digitizing of the Archival Material on Ethiopian Studies of the Frobenius Institute' project. The typewritten manuscript with the title 'Die Darassa' can be accessed in the legacy of Eike Haberland in the Frobenius Institute's archives. It is written in German and contains sixty-nine typewritten pages plus some sixty hand-written pages with additions and comments. The main chapters cover: social life, clans and dualism, the *gada* system, despised castes, religious and spiritual life, concept of God, mourning ceremonies, other ceremonies and ways of curing diseases.

4 The photos and documentaries can be found in the archives of the Frobenius Institute. See photo albums no. 013 Äthiopien (1934–35) and 027 Äthiopien (1945–55), and for the films see Ä 09, 15, 22, 30 and 76.

system and related political values; and the final section is a conclusion, containing remarks on continuities and changes among the Gedeo over the last six decades.

Study Area

During Jensen's two fieldwork trips, the Gedeo, Amaro and Guji Oromo were part of the Derasa Awraja[5] (district), in which Dilla was an administrative centre. In 1975, because of the negative connotations of the name,[6] Derasa was renamed Gedeo by the *Derg*[7] government. Then, in 1989 the *Derg* changed the country's administrative structure and Gedeo became a separate administrative zone. Finally, Gedeo became one of the zones of the Southern Nations Nationalities and Peoples Regional State (SNNPRS) with the coming to power of the Ethiopian Peoples Revolutionary Democratic Front (EPRDF). The Guji Oromo became part of the Oromia Regional State, and the Amaro became a special *woreda*[8] in the SNNPRS with the advent of ethnic-based federalism in 1991. Today's Gedeo zone is geographically smaller than the previous Gedeo district.

The Gedeo zone is bounded by the Sidama zone of the SNNPRS to the north and the Borana zone of the Oromia Regional State to the south, east and west. Dilla, the capital of Gedeo, is situated 365 kilometres south of Addis Ababa. The total area of the zone is 1,210.89 square kilometres and it is divided into six *woredas* and two city council administrations (Getachew 2017).

At the time of Jensen's fieldwork, the Gedeo lands were green and covered with agroforestry. The photos and documentary films made by Jensen show the territory covered with trees and different plantations, mainly of ensete. As Jensen stated, the region became involved in the international coffee market in the 1930s.[9] As a result, the expansion of coffee as a cash crop in the area changed the complexion of Gedeo's agriculture. Coffee plantations continued to expand at the expense of ensete plantations, and in 2012/13 coffee constituted 41 per cent of cultivated land in Gedeo zone (Getachew 2014: 126).

Jensen did not give a figure for the Gedeo population because there was no statistical data available at that time. However, he gave us a clue about population density in the area by explaining that the Gedeo land was highly populated compared to the neighbouring Sidama territory. In the 1950s there was no grazing land, except in some smaller places in Dumerso, because of population pressure and a general shortage of land.[10] Those Gedeo who owned cattle at the time had to send them to the Guji area.

According to a 2014 Central Statistics Agency (CSA) report, the population of the zone was projected to be 1,054,764 in 2015, the majority of which (81.5 per cent) lived in rural areas, with only 18.5 per cent living in urban areas (CSA 2014). Six decades after Jensen's fieldwork, Gedeo is still one of the most densely populated areas in the country.

5 *Awraja* was an administrative structure below the province. At the time Derasa Awraja was under the Sidamo Province.

6 During the imperial period, the term Derasa that referred to the Gedeo was associated with "uncivilized people" who did not have equal socioeconomic status with the ruling elites and the urban population in the towns of Gedeo.

7 *Derg* is the abbreviation for the military regime that ruled Ethiopia from 1974 to 1991.

8 An administrative structure under the zone and above the *kebele*.

9 EH-70-001:2.

10 EH-70-001:2.

According to the 2014 CSA report, the estimated population density in 2015 was 871.1 persons/km^2 (CSA 2014).[11] In some places like Mekonesa Kebele, the crude density in 2012 was as high as 1,823 persons/km^2 (Getachew 2014: 58).

The name 'Gedeo' is directly related to the people's language Gede'uffa, which is one of the Eastern Cushitic languages and has similarities with other highland Eastern Cushitic languages like Sidama, Hadiyya, Kembata and Alaba (Fleming and Bender 1976: 45). The history of the Gedeo people, mainly transmitted orally for generations, is not well studied. According to oral tradition, Derasso, Boru (the founding father of the Borana Oromo) and Urago or Gujo (the founding father of the Guji Oromo) were brothers who were descended from the same unknown father. The tradition further explains that Derasso was the eldest son, followed by Boru and then by Urago. During my own research, elderly informants explained that the respect Derasso attained from his two brothers, stemmed from his seniority (Getachew 2014: 62).

In different parts of his field notes Jensen discusses the Gedeo's relationship with the Sidama, with whom they were on friendly terms. He also mentions that the Gedeo and Guji were friendly and shared strong economic and cultural links.[12] Indeed, in my own research, I found that those Gedeo who live in the areas close to the Guji Oromo speak Oromiffa and share more similar words with Oromiffa than with Sidamigna (Getachew 2014: 62). However, in 1991, when the ethnic-based federal state structure was put in place, the Gedeo and Sidama were placed under the Southern National Nationalities and Peoples' Regional State, while the Guji became part of the Oromia Regional State. Moreover, the 1995 conflicts between the Gedeo and the Guji, caused by border and resource issues, had negative implications for the historically friendly relations between the two peoples, described by Jensen. The conflicts checked southward expansion and movement of the Gedeo and, according to some informants, suspicions developed between the two neighbouring societies.

Religion

Considering them to be of anthropological importance, Jensen described the religion and spiritual life of the Gedeo. During his fieldwork, both in 1934/5 and 1955, followers of the traditional belief system were in the majority. In the Gedeo traditional belief system, Mageno (lit. 'Sky God') is the Supreme Being (Getachew 2014: 70). According to Jensen, Mageno is male and resides in heaven.[13] Jensen mentions that there were no Muslim Gedeo during his fieldwork in 1955, but there were followers of Sheik Hussein.[14] According to Jensen, they came together on Fridays for a weekly ritual and claimed that they had inherited healing spirits from their parents.[15]

The first attempt to introduce the Gedeo to world religion came in 1896, when Orthodox Christianity was introduced following Menelik II's expansion and the in

11 The national average at the same time was 78 persons/km^2 (CSA 2014).

12 EH-70-001:2.

13 EH-70-001.

14 Sheik Hussein was an Islamic religious leader in the Bale Oromo area, who had non-Muslim followers who believed in his spirits. EH-70-001: 68.

15 EH-70-001: 68–69.

corporation of the Gedeo by the central Christian government. However, the spread of Christianity was limited, despite the fact that Emperor Haile Selassie I advocated the conversion of the Gedeo to Orthodox Christianity. One of the major reasons for the slow expansion of Orthodox Christianity was that the preaching was done in *Ge'ez* (the language used by the Ethiopian Orthodox Church) and/or in *Amharic*, which were difficult for the Gedeo to understand.

In 1948 there was another attempt to convert the Gedeo when Protestant Christianity was introduced to the Gedeo by the Sudanese Interior Mission. Protestant Christianity expanded rapidly due to preaching being done in Gedu'ffa, and the opening of schools in different parts of Gedeo, which promoted Bible reading. Above all, the Protestant missionaries sided with the Gedeo in their 1960 protest against the central government. However, the expansion of Protestant Christianity faced difficulties in the *Derg* period (1975–1991) because the socialist regime associated Protestant Christianity with Western imperialism. As a result, some churches were closed. Since the EPRDF government came to power in 1991, Protestant Christianity has again expanded rapidly.

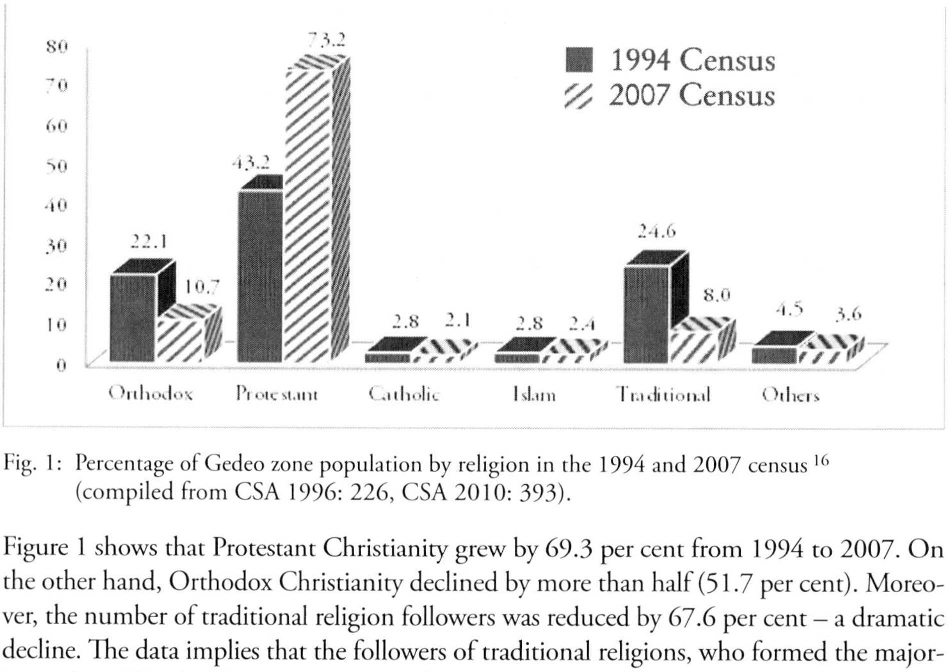

Fig. 1: Percentage of Gedeo zone population by religion in the 1994 and 2007 census [16] (compiled from CSA 1996: 226, CSA 2010: 393).

Figure 1 shows that Protestant Christianity grew by 69.3 per cent from 1994 to 2007. On the other hand, Orthodox Christianity declined by more than half (51.7 per cent). Moreover, the number of traditional religion followers was reduced by 67.6 per cent – a dramatic decline. The data implies that the followers of traditional religions, who formed the majority in the 1950s, had become a minority by 2007 census.

In addition to the basic belief system of the Gedeo, Jensen gave a detailed description of the Gedeo's burial ceremonies, partly comparing them to those of the neighbouring Sidama and Guji Oromo.[17] Death is conceptualized by the Gedeo as the time when the soul (*lubbo*) leaves the body and ascends to God. Jensen continued to explain that most people were bur-

16 The 1984 Census analytical report is based on the Sidamo region (OPHCC 1989), which covers a wider area and does not show the reality in Gedeo.

17 EH-70-001: 52–53.

ied inside their compounds. If a dead person, however, was at the *yuba*[18] stage of the Gedeo *baalle* system, he was buried outside the compound. This tradition has changed because of the expansion of Protestant Christianity. I observed during fieldwork that most people were buried in a church graveyard, as they had converted to Protestantism. Only a few elders still preferred to be buried in their compounds or fields. Traditionally, Gedeo people planted a tree on the grave of a dead person to identify the burial place, but now they have started to leave cement grave markers like those seen in Orthodox Christian burial places.

According to Jensen, the Gedeo *wodesha* (mourning ceremony) was similar to the Sidama's *wul'la*, although the Sidama ceremony was bigger.[19] The ceremony took between one and four days depending on the age, sex and status of the deceased person. There is a specific place – like the one in Mekonesa shown in Figure 2 – in each *kebele* where heroes and traditional leader's special morning ceremonies are conducted. Still, the *wodesha* ceremonies are conducted and continue to vary according to the age, sex and social status of the diseased person. However, the accompanying feasts are now much smaller due to the general decline of production in the area and are predominantly provided through the contributions of self-help associations.

Fig 2: A place where mourning ceremonies for heroes and traditional leaders are conducted in Mekonesa Kebele, 2013

18 The Gedeo *baalle* grading system has nine stages from the lowest to the highest: *qedado*, *seda*, *lumassa*, *raba*, *luba*, *yuba*, *guduro*, *qulullo* and *chewajja* (Getachew 2014: 77).

19 Jensen even provides us with a film on mourning ceremonies among the Gedeo and Sidama, both of which are no longer practised today due to the influence of Protestant Christianity (see archives no Ä 22).

The Gedeo religion also relates to livelihoods. There were, Jensen noted, special gods for specific issues in the Gedeo belief system,[20] and different prayers and rituals related to the production system from cultivation to harvest. One of the important ceremonies described by Jensen is the *dalla* ceremony, undertaken at the gate of a house or compound.[21] Once a year, the Gedeo kill a sheep on the gate as a sacrifice for a good harvest, animal health or to avoid disease. However, this ritual is no longer practised due to the expansion of Protestant Christianity and a decline in the number of livestock, caused by a shortage of land. Jensen also mentioned *qeexala*, a ritual and dance conducted for a number of ecological problems, like a shortage of rain or outbreak of locusts.[22] Again, the ritual is practised less often today because of the expansion of Christianity. Most people conduct church prayers for such ecological problems, so the number of people who attend the traditional *qeexala* ritual has reduced dramatically.

Theft was common in Gedeo during my fieldwork, especially during the coffee harvest season. Most people have established a small hut on their coffee farmland so that they can look after their crop. However some individuals put magical objects called *tarre* in their fields to protect them from theft. The Gedeo believe that if somebody steals from these fields, they may be infected by disease or struck by lightning. Jensen noted that theft of different crops from the fields was a problem in Gedeo even in the 1950s and he also described different types of *tarre* used by the farmers to protect their farms.[23]

One ceremony not mentioned by Jensen[24] is the *deraro* ritual, which is conducted at village level to thank Mageno for a new harvest. For a long time, the ritual did not take place because of the expansion of Protestant Christianity and subsequently because of the socialist *Derg* government. However, over the last ten years, the ceremony has been celebrated again as part of a revitalization movement instigated by the zone's Tourism and Culture Office (Getachew 2014: 182).

In general, most of the rituals that were described by Jensen have declined due to the expansion of Protestant Christianity. According to informants, Protestant Christianity associates most rituals with 'evil' sprit. The decline of rituals has negatively affected some of the Gedeo's cultural values. For instance, traditionally rituals were conducted with the leadership of elders. Today, youths who can read the Bible become religious teachers and leaders. In this way formal education and knowledge have become substitutes for seniority, experience and cultural knowledge. This change has negative implications for the leadership role of elders and the transfer of indigenous knowledge to the next generation.

Baalle System

In the social life section of his manuscript, Jensen discusses three interrelated issues: clans and moieties, the *baalle* system, and grading in the *baalle* system. Like most researchers in Gedeo, he identified seven clans and two moieties.[25] This classification system is

20 EH-70-001: 50.

21 EH-70-001: 55–56.

22 EH-70-001: 58–59.

23 EH-70-001:59–60.

24 Maybe because of his absence during the harvest season.

25 The two moieties in Gedeo are referred to as *baxxe*, which literally means 'house'.

still used by the Gedeo, who explain that they have two *baxxe* (houses) of exogamous moieties and seven clans. However, the importance of the two houses when making marriage arrangements had already started to decline in Jensen's day and, nowadays, it is very conmen for marriages to be arranged between two people from the same *baxxe*, but from different clans.

Jensen argued that the Gedeo adopted the *baalle* system from the neighbouring Guji Oromo. There is an ongoing debate about how the Gedeo adopted the *baalle* system. Solomon (2009) and Taddesse et al. (2008) argue that the Gedeo *baalle* system is indigenous to the Gedeo. According to them, the Gedeo people developed it after the *gossalo*[26] clan-based rule. On the other hand, Asebe (2007) and McClellan (1988) argue, like Jensen, that the Gedeo adopted the *baalle* system from the neighbouring Guji Oromo, though they present different stories on the process of adoption.

Both sides in the debate over whether the *baalle* system is indigenous or adopted cite evidence that supports their point of view and devalue facts that are against it. It seems possible, and indeed plausible, that the Gedeo adopted the *baalle* system from the neighbouring Guji Oromo since the fact that the Guji have a higher number of former *abba gadas* (leader of the *gada* age grade system) than the Gedeo suggests that the *gada* system of the Oromo was in place for longer than the Gedeo *baalle* system. However, the Gedeo might have adopted the system based on their situational needs and modified it for centuries. As a result, they indigenized the *baalle* system and it became a marker of their identity.

Jensen's explanation of the *baalle* grading system, especially the transfer process and generation succession, was clearer than that offered by any other researcher who has since worked on it.[27] In addition, he was the only researcher to observe and document the last *baalle* grade transfer ceremony, performed in 1955. He also observed a special *baalle* grade transition hunting expedition undertaken by the *rabas* (members of the *raba* age grade) of Belibeba *baalle* and led by those from each district who held the positions of *murite* and *bobbassa*.[28] The hunters sang and chanted about their heroic deeds, they established a camp and unmarried girls were responsible for supplying them with food; any *rabas* who stayed at home were considered women.[29]

Jensen identified only seven grades in the Gedeo *baalle* system: *lumassa, raba, luba, yuba, guduro, qulullo,* and *chewajja*.[30] However, nine *baalle* grades have been identified by Getachew (2014) and Tadesse et al. (2008). These are, from the lowest to the highest: *qedado, seda, lumassa, raba, luba, yuba, guduro, qulullo* and *chewajja*. In the Gedeo *baalle* system, a son is always two grades behind his father, meaning that they are in the same class. All sons of a single father are in the same grade; hence the grading system is not purely an age-grade system. That is why Jensen commented that it was strange to

26 According to oral tradition, the *gossalo* rule, which succeeded the *akkomalo* matriarchal administration, was the clan-based administration before the introduction of the *baalle* system in Gedeo (Getachew 2014: 74).

27 EH-70-001:24.

28 A *baalle* that came to power in the 1955 transition.

29 EH-70-001:28–29.

30 EH-70-001:24.

see a younger person at the *luba* stage and an older person in the *raba* (junior) stage.[31] A younger man in the *luba* stage takes priority over an older man in the *raba* stage when crossing a river or taking food and drink in any ceremony.

The above-mentioned grading system was weakened during the imperial period, and most of my elderly informants argued that the campaign Jensen described and photographed was the last real *baalle* grade transition. It has not been practised since then due to political pressure from the central government, which considers the *baalle* system as a competitor to governmental power, and the expansion of Protestant Christianity, which rejects any rituals and sacrifices related to the traditional belief system.

During the *Derg* period (1975–1991) the government discouraged the practise of any religious rituals or traditional administration system that contradicted socialist ideology and administration. After the downfall of the *Derg* and the coming to power of the EPRDF government, the freedom to partake in cultural ceremonies became a constitutional right, and a considerable number of ethnic groups tried to revive some of their traditional practices in a modified way that harmonized with the current situation and government development policy in the area. The Gedeo tried to revive some of their traditional practices, but not the grading system, and most Gedeo do not like to participate in the rituals and sacrifices that relate to grade transfer.

Jensen reported that the Gedeo political organization also emanated from the *gada/baalle* system. He mentioned that the *abba gada*, *ja'laba* (deputy for the *abba gada*), *murite* (justice), *fetich* (administrator), *bobbassa* (speaker) and *hayichas* (elders) took office when they reached the *raba* stage and that the land of Gedeo was divided into three *roga* (zones): Suuboo *roga* (highland located in the east), Dhibata *roga* (west-midland), and Riiqata *roga* (lowland in the south). Each *roga* was ruled by a leader, also called a *roga* (leader), and his deputy, the *jalqaba*. The lowest local administrative unit under the *roga* was the *songo* – a ritual and public place at the village level, where court cases were decided and other decisions made. Jensen explained that in twenty minutes walking he came across three *songos*, and that each was served by three *hayichas* and between one and three *muras*, who acted as messengers for the *hayicha* and transmit information between the people and the *hayicha*.[32]

Jensen argued that this political organization was intact up to the coming of the Amhara in the late nineteenth century.[33] When the central Christian government took control of the Gedeo area, they established their own administration system and it was gradually strengthened over the next years. During the imperial period the administration system had not yet reached the grassroots level, unlike the *baalle* system in which *songos* are found at the village level. For instance, one *balabat* (governor) might have controlled three or four *kebeles* in the imperial period, whereas between four and six *songos* might be found in a *kebele*. Therefore, the *songos* were more accessible to the local community, and most minor cases were resolved through the *baalle* system.

According to informants, a real change came during the *Derg* period, when the current *kebeles*, which have an administrative role, were established under the name of Peasant Associations. In addition, there were elected judges (*fird shengo*) to resolve minor

31 EH-70-001:27.

32 EH-70-001:43–46.

33 EH-70-001:46.

cases. Still, the *songos* remained more accessible and less formal. However, the *Derg* government obliged local people to resolve their cases through the formal Peasant Association's *fird shengo*. Moreover, the successions of the *abba gada* and other positions in the *baalle* system were interrupted during the *Derg* period.

After the collapse of the *Derg* government in 1991 and the establishment of Gedeo as an administrative unit in the area, the Gedeo tried to revitalize succession. The *abba gada* election was reinstituted during the EPRDF period in 1993 and *abba gada* Qnaqe, *abba gada* Gelibo, *abba gada* Shiferaw Miidhe and *abba gada* Shallo Bosha have since been elected consecutively from specific clans, according to the traditional succession rules. Similarly, *roga* successions have been established again. In addition, 525 *songos* have been reinstituted and the use of the *songos* in resolving minor disputes is acknowledged. However, the real power of the *baalle* has not yet been reinstituted. Despite these efforts the former Peasant Associations become *kebeles* and the *fird shengo* become *mahiberaw fird bet* (social court), tasked with resolving minor cases in a more formal ways. Furthermore, under the *kebele* there are sub-*kebeles*, which suggest that the governmental administrative structure has reached the grassroots or family level in Gedeo more than ever before. This has negative implications for the role of traditional administration in the day-to-day lives of the Gedeo. The Gedeo *baalle* system has become more of a symbol. Today, the *baalle* administration and political system has weakened to such an extent that it does not play a significant role in the lives of the Gedeo in spite of the efforts made by the Gedeo Zone Culture Office to revitalize some of its elements.[34]

Conclusion

Jensen gave us the earliest comparative ethnographic account of the Gedeo people. Overall, the valuable material in Jensen's ethnographic work provides a useful basis for further insights and understanding of the dynamics of the two important and interrelated institutions, religion and the *baalle* system, in the life of the Gedeo. His documentation – in written, pictorial, and audio-visual form – provides important data for the attempt to understand changes and continuities among the Gedeo. We have seen that the Gedeo lands have gained new internal dynamics with the cultivation of coffee, but the tradition of maintaining agroforestry has been continued. Most of the people's religious practices have changed over the last six decades due to the introduction and expansion of Protestant Christianity and the interruptions by the imperial and socialist regimes. Although some traditional practices have continued, albeit on a lower scale and with some modification, the decline of traditional rituals has considerably weakened the Gedeo *baalle* system, since grade transfer is based on rituals and traditional religion was used as a reinforcement mechanism for the *baalle* system. Moreover, the establishment of the central government administration system in the area devalued the administrative roles of the *baalle* system. Thus, the Gedeo *baalle* system functions today largely only as a symbol of Gedeo identity.

34 The EPRDF government policy selectively promotes cultural expressions that do not contradict with the government development policy. Epple and Thubauville (2012) highlight the contradiction between the promotion of cultural diversity and national development, or tradition and modernity, since the coming to power of the EPRDF government in 1991 in which pressure and induced cultural changes observed in Southern Nations, Nationalities and People Region.

References

ASEBE Regasa

2007 *Ethnicity and inter-ethnic relations: The 'Ethiopian experiment' and the case of the Guji and Gedeo.* MPhil Thesis, University of Tromsø, Norway.

CENTRAL STATISTICS AGENCY (CSA)

1996 *The 1994 population and housing census of Ethiopia results from Southern Nations, Nationalities and Peoples' Region.* Vol. I, Part I. Addis Ababa: Central Statistics Agency.

2010 *The 2007 population and housing census of Ethiopia result for Southern Nations, Nationalities and Peoples' Region.* Addis Ababa: Central Statistics Agency.

2014 *Population statistical abstract.* Addis Ababa: Central Statistics Agency.

EPPLE, Susanne and Sophia THUBAUVILLE

2012 'Cultural diversity in Ethiopia between appreciation and suppression', *Paideuma* 58: 153–166.

FLEMING, Harold C. and Marvin L. BENDER

1976 'Cushitic and Omotic', in: M.L. BENDER, J.D. BOWEN, R.L. COOPER, and C.A. FERGUSON (eds.): *Language in Ethiopia*, 34–53. London: Oxford University Press.

GETACHEW Senishaw

2014 *The nexus of indigenous ecological knowledge, livelihood strategies and social institutions in Midland Gedeo human-environment relations.* PhD Dissertation, Addis Ababa University.

2017 'The Gedeo, Adolf Ellegard Jensen's ethnographic perspective', in: Sabine DINSLAGE and Sophia THUBAUVILLE (eds.): *Seeking out wise old men. Six decades of Ethiopian Studies at the Frobenius Institute revisited*, 265-282. Berlin: Reimer.

JENSEN, Adolf Ellegard

1936 *Im Lande des Gada. Wanderungen zwischen Volkstrümmern Südabessiniens.* Stuttgart: Strecker & Schröder.

MCCLELLAN, Charles

1988 *State transformation and national integration: Gedeo and the Ethiopian Empire, 1895–1935.* East Lansing: Michigan State University.

SOLOMON Hailu

2009 *History of the Gedeo, 1941–2000.* MA Thesis, Addis Ababa University.

TADESSE Kippie, Tilahun EBIDO, Tsegay TADESSE, Hayilu BEYENE and Shinitu LLOE

2008 *Ye GedeoBiher Tarek.* Addis Ababa: Berhanena Selam Printing Press.

WOHLENBERG, Hellmut

1988 *Im südlichen Abessinien. Reiseberichte von Oktober 1934 bis Mai 1935.* Hildesheim: Olms.

Craftworkers, Hunters and Slave Descendants in Ethiopia

New Perspectives on the Dynamics of Social Categories

SUSANNE EPPLE

Introduction

The distinctive and often low status of occupation and descent-based groups is a worldwide phenomenon, still found particularly in South Asia and many parts of Africa.[1] Different disciplines, such as history, social anthropology and political science, have studied the scope, underlying causes, local explanations and justifications for the social exclusion many such groups experience. More recently, their lived experience as well as the dynamics around the boundaries between the social categories have become of interest, partly because members of such groups have begun to speak out. In some countries, such as India or Nigeria, concerned activist groups have addressed social exclusion based on occupation or descent and have recently begun to draw national and international attention to the issue.[2]

In Ethiopia, the present and previous governments have made many efforts to establish equality and integration of excluded groups. Today, churches run numerous awareness-raising programmes and some national and international NGOs and activist groups are also active in the country (Freeman and Pankhurst 2001).[3] Yet, as many studies show, marginalization continues to exist. Some authors (for example, Aalen 2011, 2012; Tronvoll and Hagmann 2012) even report that due to the high value given to local values and cultural practices in the context of ethnic federalism, marginalization of craft workers, hunters and slave descendants has been revitalized.

For a long time, the vast literature on Ethiopian occupation and descent-based groups emphasized their marginalization. Many early publications described their origin, history and livelihood as well as the scope and kind of their marginalization, and often compared them with Indian castes. More recently, researchers have begun to look at the flexibility of social categories and the redefinition of social boundaries between dominant herders and farmers and submissive craft workers, hunters and slave descendants.

This paper examines the existing literature with a special focus on the dynamics around the boundaries between dominant majorities and different status groups.

1 According to Pinto (2001: 2817, 2002: 3988), there are more than 260 million people (most of them Dalits – untouchables – from India) suffering from descent and occupation-based exclusion in the world.

2 See, for example, the Asia Dalit Forum, an activist group fighting for equal treatment and chances for Indian Dalits and similar groups in other countries (http://asiadalitrightsforum.org/interventions.php).

3 See, for example, the work of KMG Ethiopia in Kembatta (also: Kambata), which fights for gender equality, and end to FGM (female genital mutilation), and the empowerment of the locally marginalized 'Fuga' (craftworkers) (http://kmgethiopia.org).

Occupation and Descent-Based Status Groups in Ethiopia

Common to all occupation and descent-based groups is their distinctive, often disadvantaged position, which is ascribed by birth and passed on through generations. Usually, it is locally justified by a state of pollutedness (physical or ritual) believed to cause disease and misfortune for others and that is, in some cases, transmittable to others through close contact.

In Ethiopia, occupational groups (mostly potters, tanners, weavers, blacksmiths, woodworkers, certain musicians), hunters (and descendants of hunters), slave descendants, ethnic splinters and some special clans find themselves living under similar conditions. Living either as part of a society with inner differentiation or close to a dominant group (mostly farmers or, in some cases, pastoralists or agro-pastoralists), they are found in stratified as well as rather egalitarian societies in almost all parts of Ethiopia. Usually excluded from the activities of the dominant sections of the society, often disadvantaged, and sometimes discriminated against, such groups have been referred to in the literature with terms such as 'avoided castes', 'pariah', 'outcasts', 'depressed classes' or 'marginalized groups'.[4] However, there exists a great variation in the kinds of relationship these groups entertain with the dominant sections of society, as well as with each other.

Perceived Characteristics

Occupational groups (craftworkers, hunters), slave descendants and similar groups are usually perceived as being fundamentally different from the mainstream society. While craftworkers, hunters and certain musicians often play an ambiguous role – with both negative and positive attributes – the status of slave descendants is marked solely by notions of inferiority.

Among the shared alleged negatives characteristics of occupational groups and slave descendants are physical and/or ritual impurity, an unsocial and disloyal character and, in some cases, racial difference to the majority. In Ethiopia – and elsewhere – these attributes are explained and justified mainly by: (1) polluting professions or activities and/or the handling of impure materials;[5] (2) mythical origins such as descent from unions between humans and animals; (3) loss of pure human status through ancestors' improper or immoral behaviour or through an ancestral curse; and (4) loss of proper human status through becoming a slave.

4 The term 'caste' used to be commonly employed in the literature on Ethiopia. But it has also been debated for several reasons, including the fact that the term caste implies more parallels between the Ethiopian context and the Indian caste system than some authors believe exist (for the discussion on the term see Todd 1977; Amborn 1990; Pankhurst 1999). Some authors have opted for more neutral terms, such as 'status groups' (Amborn 1990), 'hereditary status groups' (Ellison 2006) or 'cultural strata' (Braukämper 2014).

5 Crafts are often considered as impure activities as they imply contact with impure materials and substances, such as dead animals and animal skins, or the handling of dangerous materials, such as fire and metal. Hunters touch and consume the allegedly impure meat of wild game and are generally associated with the wilderness, rather than with culture. In many cases, craftworkers, hunters and members of special clans are given responsibility for social duties such as circumcision, washing and burying the dead, digging graves and the like, which contributes to their pollutedness.

Among the alleged positive or special characteristics of craftworkers and hunters are special powers and abilities to bless, to curse and to heal. In many societies, craftworkers and hunters were afforded indispensable roles related to the 'social reproduction of the dominant society' (Pankhurst 2001: 2): as assistants or key persons during life-cycle events, such as initiation rituals, circumcisions, births or funerals (Pankhurst 2001: 1–2). Some of these activities are locally considered as dangerous or polluting.

In some societies, hunters have been used as mediators in conflict resolution among the dominant sections of society, and as assistants of the ritual king. As such, they had to execute those who were condemned to death, act as the king's guardians and protect the sacred fire and the king's insignia, bury him when he died and initiate a new one (Haberland 1962, 1964). Craftworkers were also important as producers of goods necessary for daily life as well as for ritual purposes. Slaves played an important economic role in many societies, yet they were not accorded any respect for this and there are no reports of slave descendants having any ritual or social responsibilities (Epple 2018).

Representation in the Early Literature

Craftworkers, hunters and slave descendants were mentioned in very early publications on Ethiopia (Cerulli 1922, Pankhurst 1961), but those written by members of the Frobenius Institute provide the first detailed overview.

The Frobenius Institute organized four expeditions to southern Ethiopia in 1934–35, 1950–52 and 1954–56. These resulted in the publication of four large volumes (Jensen 1936, 1959; Straube 1963; Haberland 1963)[6] that gave detailed descriptions of the history and culture of many of the groups they had visited, many of which were internally highly differentiated. Extra chapters or subchapters were dedicated to the description of marginalized subgroups,[7] including occupational groups, hunters and slave descendants, as well as special clans. There was a focus on providing a description of their alleged origins, their livelihood activities, their ambiguous roles and duties and their relationship with dominant sections of the societies in or near which they lived. Eike Haberland later went into more detail and published articles and books on the extraordinary relationship between 'pariah groups' and 'sacred kings' (Haberland 1964) as well as on hunters and special castes (Haberland 1962), slavery in Woleyta (Haberland 1992), and the highly stratified society of the Dizi people (Haberland 1984, 1993). His student Werner Lange wrote about divine kingship and the special position of bards in Kaffa (Lange 1976, 1979/80).

In the decades after the Frobenius's expeditions, many monographs on Ethiopian societies with marginalized subgroups appeared (see Shack 1966; Teclehaimanot 2003 on the *fuga* in Gurage; Hallpike 1972 on *xauda* in Konso; Huntingford 1955 on Manjo in Kaffa; Gamst 1979 on Wayto in Amhara; Quirin 1979 on Beta Israel in Amhara

6 There are also unpublished manuscripts at the Frobenius Institute describing some of these groups in detail. See, for example, the material on the Sidama, Woleyta and Gede'o, which has recently been reviewed by Ambaye (2017), Data (2017) and Getachew (2017).

7 Some of the names used in the older literature for ethnic groups are designations by other groups and/or names nowadays considered as outdated or derogatory. In this article, therefore, I have decided to use the currently acceptable names.

in Tigray). These detailed accounts showed how differentiated and stratified internally many Ethiopian societies are, and they emphasized the existing marginalization and strict social boundaries between minorities and majorities. However, a close inspection of the material provides some indications that the boundaries between these categories were not as rigid as is often assumed.

Internal Differentiation and Stratifications

'Assimilated' members of society

Various Oromo groups (such as Borana, Arsi, Guji) and also some non-Oromo groups (Gede'o and Yem) differentiate their population into 'real/original' and 'assimilated' members (Haberland EH70: 18ff; Straube 1963: 305ff; Haberland 1963: 127). Intermarriage between original and assimilated members of society was reportedly originally forbidden and assimilated members were also not allowed to take any public office. According to Haberland (1963: 129), this differentiation had already either been overcome or at least become less important in some places. Various Oromo groups allowed intermarriage in the 1950s, for example, but still restricted participation in the Gada-system.

Craftworkers

Rules of endogamy and avoidance between farmers and craftworkers, as well as between different craftworkers and towards hunters and slave descendants, exist in many Ethiopian societies (Jensen 1959; Haberland 1963; Freeman and Pankhurst 2001). Avoidance includes commensality, close physical contact (especially sexual intercourse), as well as entering each other's houses and touching each other's objects (especially food containers, dishes and tools). Most authors emphasize the prohibitions set by the majority. However, the avoidance can work both ways: craftworkers do not necessarily allow farmers to enter their compounds and touch their work tools. Most commonly known in the literature on craftworkers are the *hadicho* in Woleyta (Aalen 2011), the *manni* in Ari (Jensen 1959; Schulz-Weidner 1959; Straube 1963), the *manna* among some groups neighbouring the Ari (see Straube 1963 on Amarro; Behailu and Data 2003 on Dawro; Dereje 2001 on Oyda) and the *hauda* in Konso (Hallpike 1968; Amborn 1990; Watson 2006).

Hunters, descendants of hunters

Close interaction with hunters is often avoided as they are considered to be impure, often due to their consumption of wild game and other 'unclean' meat.[8] Among the well-known hunter groups are the *fuga* in Gurage (Shack 1966; Teclehaimanot 2003), the *Weyto* in Amhara, the *Manjo* in Kaffa (Huntingford 1955; Gezaghn 2003), and the *Wata* in Borana (Haberland 1963) and among other Oromo groups. In some former kingdoms, hunters had certain responsibilities considered as impure (for example, washing corpses and digging graves). They also performed ritual and social services for the mainstream society or the king/ritual leaders; for example, as assistants in rites of pas-

8 Meat is considered impure if it either comes from impure animals (typically hippopotamus and other wild game), from dead animals or from animals that are slaughtered in a way considered as polluting. The latter is especially relevant in Orthodox Christianity and Islam.

sage, performers of purifying rituals (Haberland 1962, 1964) and mediators in conflict resolution (Gemeda 2016).

Slave descendants

Slavery was officially abolished in 1942 under Haile Selassie,[9] but slave identity continues to be passed on to the next generation or through close contact. Descendants of slaves continue to be distinguished from those descended from the freeborn. Intermarriage with farmers and craftworkers is often prohibited and close contact avoided.[10] There is little literature on slaves (Haberland on Woleyta 1992) and even less on slave descendants (see Olmstead 1973 on Gamo; Bosha 2013, 2018 on Ganta; and Kiya 2018 on the Rayya Qobo highlands, Amhara).

Special clans/members of religious group

Other groups distinct and excluded from the mainstream society include the Beta Israel (also Falasha) the Ethiopian Jewish community despised for its religious beliefs (Haberland 1962; Quirin 1979) and believed to have the evil eye; splinters of other groups, such as the Kumpal Agaw, believed to be afflicted by an ancestral curse (Desalegn 2018); and special clans or subgroups, such as the *bajje* people living among the Hamar who are considered to be impure but responsible for rites of passage among the majority (Epple 2010)[11].

Internal Dynamics and Culture Immanent Mechanisms for Change

In the Frobenius Institute's publications, the impossibility of moving out of the status group one was born into is repeatedly mentioned. Yet, a closer reading of the available descriptions reveals that options for change did and do exist for both individuals and subgroups. In the following, examples from the early literature will be presented and partly complemented by more recent work of other researchers.

Marriage and adoption

The prohibition on intermarriage is one of the strongest and most persistent rules separating occupational groups, slave descendants and farmers from each other. Yet, there are

9 The attempt to eliminate slavery began in 1923 when Emperor Haile Selassie was asked to abolish slavery as a precondition for admittance to the League of the Nations (Smidt 2010). In 1936, during the Italian occupation, a proclamation of the general liberation of all slaves was issued (Braukämper 2014: 79), yet authors claim that slavery continued in parts of the country. After the Italian occupation, the Emperor issued a new proclamation (in 1942) abolishing any form of slave trade and the legal institution of slavery itself.

10 The most prominent example of this is found among the Woleyta people, whose slaves at times consisted of around 30 per cent of the total Woleyta population and who were differentiated into numerous subcategories (Haberland 1992).

11 The *bajje* constitute a special group who is said to have come from Ari. They live in small families in Hamar and Banna and do not perform their rituals or intermarry with them. Yet, they perform a key rite of passage for young married couples as well as some cleansing rituals for women who have had a miscarriage or abortion. As such, they are venerated and despised at the same time.

reports of exceptions being made under certain conditions or for certain sections of a society. In societies where virginity is a precondition for marriage, for example, girls who lost their virginity have been married off to men from a lower status group. This was the case for Guji-Oromo girls, who were given to the neighbouring Bayso or Boroda people or to the Wata, a group of hunters with whom intermarriage was otherwise unthinkable (Haberland 1963: 328). Widowed or divorced women have also been allowed to choose a new husband from the Wata (Haberland 1963: 135).

In some societies, such as among the Konso (Ellison 2006; Amborn 1990), the strict prohibition on marrying artisans applies only to first or second born sons, who are usually responsible for rituals; subsequent sons are more free to marry across status boundaries. Among the Dirassa, intermarriage is, for some, encouraged: members of the priests' lineage prefer craftworkers as marriage partners, as they are said to have 'good and light blood' (Amborn 1990: 295).

Previously strict prohibitions have also reportedly softened between different craftworkers, hunters and slave descendants: between the Wata hunters and Borana blacksmiths (Haberland 1963: 135); and between the southern Guji and slaves who were bought from Burji or Amarro (Haberland 1963: 348). The reasons why these prohibitions were given up have yet to be explored.

Economic status can play a major role, as recent studies on Konso have shown. Here, the wealth achieved by many craftworkers recently has turned them into attractive marriage partners (Belete 2012; Ellison 2006; Kansite 2017).

Adoption, especially common among Oromo groups, is a way of integrating strangers fully into society. In Arsi, slaves could be adopted by the family that owned them (Haberland 1963: 131). The same has been shown to be true for the Alabdu-Guji people, although the rights of adopted slaves to assume any political office were regulated and restricted (Haberland 1963: 294).[12]

Changing or adopting secondary occupations

Many authors observe that, under certain circumstances, craftworkers, hunters and even farmers change profession or adopt a secondary occupation as a way of adapting to changes in the economic or natural environment (Amborn 1990; also Watson 2006). For example, in times of drought or when population pressure became too high, farmers tended to adopt additional activities, often craftwork. Jensen (1936: 104) mentioned the case of Darassa farmers who engaged in blacksmithing to earn extra income. More recently, farmers in Konso have been seen to engage in craftwork in order to supplement their income (Ellison 2006; Belete 2012). However, as Amborn (2009: 118) has remarked, this is not always in the interests of the craftworkers, as it means that they lose full control over the industry, forcing them to develop certain mechanisms for controlling the integration of farmers into their associations. Likewise, there are examples of hunters who turned to craftwork when wild game became scarce or hunting was persecuted. Straube (1963: 41) mentioned the *Bandu* hunters living among the Sheko, who became potters along with some of the dominant farmers' women.

12 If someone was adopted by the *akako* ('original' Guji), that person's descendants could take over important ritual or political offices after five generations but adoption by the *dalata* ('assimilated' Guji) did not confer the same rights.

Craftworkers have also been seen to begin to farm or engage in a secondary craft when they experience a decline in economic opportunities. Most tanners in southern Ethiopia, for example, became weavers when the Amhara occupants forbade leather clothing (Amborn 1990: 210). Such was the case among, for example, the Gede'o (Haberland EH 70).[13] In Shangama (part of Ari) (Schulz-Weidner 1959: 139) and Konso (Hallpike 1968: 269) some craftworkers became farmers to earn extra income. In recent times, since tourism has increased the demand for local products (Belete 2012), craftworkers have achieved wealth and recognition (Ellison 2006: 212).

Craftworkers have their own cultural values and prohibitions, and they disapprove of people who want to give up the craft. According to Amborn (1990: 295), first-born sons in the Konso-Burji cluster are usually obliged to continue their father's craft. The further away an individual's descent is from the main lineage, the less strictly the rules are applied. For example, among the Dirassa, the rule of sticking to the family profession is less strictly applied to junior members of the family, who are allowed to give up their craft and farm while the senior members are supposed to continue the tradition. Likewise, junior sons of farmers sometimes become artisans (Amborn 1990: 296). However, an orientation towards farming often does not imply any change in status, and can also lead to envy and the renewed marginalization of producers, as Ellison (2006) observed among the Konso.

Loss and repurchase of status in the context of slavery

Slavery and the slave trade were widespread in Ethiopia and produced different forms of social differentiation in various societies. While slaves were often captured or purchased from other groups, some societies took slaves from within their own population.

Bosha (2013) has shown how free farmers among the Ganta became slaves to their own neighbours and relatives through sudden impoverishment. Their slave status, which was strongly associated with pollution and de-humanization, continues to be transferred through the generations and to others who came into close contact with them during their rites of passage.

In Woleyta, Haberland (1961: 162–164) reported,[14] poor members of conquered groups became slaves, while rich and respected members were simply incorporated. Occasionally, members of richer families volunteered to become the king's slaves. The Woleyta king could also turn members of his own group into slaves if they transgressed norms or failed to perform ritual/religious duties. Poor and lazy farmers could also be made slaves of respected warriors if the king agreed.

Regaining free status was difficult or impossible in most cases, though redemption for some has been reported. A payment of seventeen oxen could free a slave among the

13 According to Amborn (1990: 128ff), efforts to prohibit leather clothes were made in the early twentieth century, but were only strictly enforced in many places in southern Ethiopia after the Second World War. Nowadays, leather clothes are only common among the women of a few groups in South Omo.

14 The king could turn ordinary people but not craftworkers into slaves; craftworkers were considered to be too different to become slaves (Haberland 1961: 162).

Zala[15] (Schulz-Weidner 1959: 239), and slaves in Woleyta who had reached old age could replace themselves with a substitute slave (Haberland 1961: 168). As slave identity continues to be transferred to new generations in some places, redemption is still an issue today. Among the Ganta, slave descendants are still despised but can regain full free status through a costly and complex ritual (Bosha 2013, 2014). Slave descendants in Woleyta are also still despised and it is unclear if there is a way for them to undergo redemption (Akalework 2014).

Adaptation and distancing

A strong means by which groups can change their status seems to be cultural and linguistic adaptation. In some cases this has led to a real blurring of boundaries, in others to only a superficially closer relationship between dominant majority and marginalized groups.

The early literature already noted that some marginalized groups had adapted to the dominant majority to an extent that outsiders could hardly distinguish them. The adaptations observed ranged from copying jewellery, clothing and hairstyle, to the imitation of social practices and the adoption of the dominant language.

Jensen (1959: 62) reported that *manni* (craftworkers) who lived among Baka (part of Ari) farmers copied their marriage rules and classes. The Wata hunters adapted to the Borana dress code to the extent that Eike Haberland, who lived with a Wata family for several weeks, did not notice that they were not Borana (Haberland 1963: 13). Like other Wata groups living with Oromo people, they also completely adopted the language of the Borana. The outward adaptation has not, however, led to an integration of the two groups.

Slave descendants in the Rayya Qobbo highlands of Amhara region have outwardly fully adapted to the majority group and cannot be distinguished from them by outsiders. However, internally they continue to be considered as different, and intermarriage is still prohibited (Kiya 2018). The Manjo, former hunters, gave up their own language completely and speak a variation of the language of the dominant Kafa people (Leikola 2018). While social integration between Manjo and Kafa is very limited, the Manjo have developed a way of manipulating their social status through adapting their linguistic repertoires to different situations: they put effort into copying the Kafa way of speaking when they want to emphasize unity with them (for example, when they ask something of them), and distance themselves by speaking differently when they intend to demonstrate ethnic difference (for example, when they claim special rights as a discriminated minority) (Leikola 2018). The hippo-hunting Haro adapted their culture so profoundly to their dominant neighbours, the agropastoralist Bayso, that today the two groups not only cooperate on daily basis, but even allow intermarriage: most of the Haro abandoned the consumption of hippo meat – considered as polluting by the Bayso – introduced male and female circumcision and copied ritual institutions and offices from the Bayso (Epple and Braukmann 2018). They also increasingly use Bayso language in their daily conversations not only with the Bayso but also among themselves, and imitate Bayso behaviour in code-switching to Amharic (Savà 2018).

15 Schulz-Weidner spells their name Sala. Today, they are not considered an independent group but are classified as part of the Gofa people.

In some cases, marginalized groups or sections of certain societies have tried to distance themselves from the dominant majority group – with differing success.[16] The *hadicho* (craftworkers among the Sidama) recently formed their own district and founded their own political party, thereby developing their own political voice (Aalen 2000). The *fuldo* traders (and craftworkers) association in Konso has become so strong that it has contributed to a common identity as *xauda* (craftworkers) (Watson 2006: 82). Similar movements have been observed among the so-called *fuga* craftworkers who live scattered among the Gurage, Kambata and other groups. Under Italian rule they were recognized as a distinct group and were able to participate politically for a short period of time (Teclehaimanot 2003). The attempts of slave descendants (*ayle*) in Ganta to physically distance themselves from the dominant majority led to conflict between them and the farmers (*malla*) that went on until the *ayle* were convinced to reunite with the *malla* (Bosha 2018).

Increased internal differentiation

A side effect of cultural and linguistic adaptation can be increased differentiation within marginalized groups. Haberland (1963: 135) reported that in the 1950s only some of the Wata had adapted to Borana culture. Those who had changed referred to themselves as *warana*-Wata (lit.: spear-Wata), referring to the fact that they had abandoned their traditional weapons in favour of the Borana spear. Those who continued to hunt with bows and arrows called themselves *tiya*-Wata (lit.: arrow-Wata). The two Wata subgroups stopped intermarrying, but the social boundaries between them and the Borana persisted. Schulz-Weidner (1959: 240) reported that Zala blacksmiths who had abandoned their craft in favour of farming were no longer allowed to marry those who continued smithing. Among the Konso, many members of the *fuldo* trade converted to Orthodox Christianity, which helped them find shelter and support among Christians when they travelled to other parts of the country. However, it also led to some fragmentation among the Konso, between those who became Protestants and those who continued to follow traditional beliefs (Watson 2006: 84)

Urban context as a place to hide one's identity

Urban contexts and places with ethnic mixing seem to offer better chances for the integration of marginalized people as personal identity and descent are much easier to cover there and such places allow individuals to distance themselves from the local context. Jensen (1936: 39) already indicated this in the 1930s. For slave descendants in the Rayya Qobbo highlands, for example, this was the only way they could hide and then change their status (Kiya 2018) and the same is true for the Manja in Kaffa Zone (Vaughan 2003: 279).

Legitimacy and self-perpetuation of marginalization

In general, the dominant majority resists the integration of the alleged impure. How-

16 In order to attain political rights, the Waata hunters of northern Kenya are trying to be acknowledged as an independent ethnic group (Aneesa 2000; Aneesa and Ali 2004). In Somalia, occupational groups have deliberately formed a new identity to increase their chances of being acknowledged as persecuted refugees (Hoehne 2014).

ever, there are some cases of minorities also resisting integration and some in which the minority itself actively contributes to the sustaining of social separation. We have already seen that the admission of farmers into the *fuldo* association of the Konso was not easily accepted and not welcomed by all (Amborn 2018). Meckelburg (2018) has also indicated that not only do the memories of their superiority survive in the minds of former slave masters, but also that the Mao and Komo themselves have deeply internalized the feelings of humiliation and marginalization they experienced in the past. Desalegn (2018) shows how, for centuries, the Kumpal's belief in an ancestral curse has contributed to their failure to overcome their precarious situation.

Recent Research: Changes through External Efforts

Much of the recent literature focuses on external measures taken to bring about change and more equality between farmers/herders and occupational groups and slave descendants, some of which were mentioned sporadically in the earlier literature. They broadly include: political intervention by the government; religious conversion; economic environment; and social factors.

Political intervention

Under various Ethiopian regimes, new laws and policies relating to land ownership, the rights of ethnic groups and individual citizens, to human rights and participation have had a clear impact on the status of minorities and hereditary status groups.

Many southern Ethiopian groups lost their independence due to their incorporation into the Ethiopian Empire under Menelik II at the end of the nineteenth century. They had to reorganize their social structures because northern settlers were often placed at the top of local hierarchies and/or local kings and ritual leaders were employed as tax collectors and intermediaries between government and local population. While central government policy did not address the social differentiation directly, the depopulation that followed conquest in some areas, as well as high taxes and tributes, meant that farmers could not produce enough food for the whole population anymore. Thus, the strict division of labour between farmers and craftworkers could not be upheld and some craftworkers had to take up farming as either a side business or as their only business (Amborn 1990: 57).

Trade was intensified by the road building undertaken during the Italian occupation and later under Haile Selassie, and this posed new challenges for craftworkers. Scrap metal, for example, became more easily accessible, which resulted a decline in iron smelting, and new products from the north and from abroad began to compete with local goods (Pankhurst and Freeman 2001: 334). Emperor Haile Selassie's efforts to modernize Ethiopia, particularly through investment in modern education and the elimination of slavery in 1942, created new opportunities for many marginalized people. However, authors have stated that negative images and stereotypes about slave descendants continue to persist (see, for example, Aalen 2012; Akalework 2014; Bosha 2013, 2014; Meckelburg 2015).

The socialist *Derg* regime (1974–1991) under Prime Minister Mengistu Haile Mariam promoted equal recognition and chances for all citizens (Donham 1999: 129f) through efforts to eliminate traditional belief systems and the unequal social structures responsible for social exclusion. The 1975 land reform allowed craftworkers and slave descendants to produce their own food and thereby improve their social standing, although this did not lead to a redefinition of their status (Pankhurst and Freeman 2001: 342). The villagization programme forced marginalized groups and farmers to live side-by-side in cooperative villages. Education was made accessible for all and craftworkers, slave descendants and hunters were given political positions in local administrative offices and in farmers' cooperative organizations (Pankhurst and Freeman 2001: 335). The population was instructed to ignore social, ethnic, religious and other differences, discriminatory behaviour was forbidden and commensality in some cases even enforced at gunpoint (Yoshida 2018). Conversion to Orthodox Christianity was suggested to some marginalized groups as a way of improving relationships with the dominant majorities. Recent literature indicates that the imposition of these rules by the *Derg* did not bring the expected results everywhere, were only superficially achieved and were unsustainable. Indeed, treatment by the dominant sections of societies changed only superficially and, due to discrimination, many members of excluded groups discontinued their education, continued to be disadvantaged in employment and political participation, and were often given small, poor quality plots of land (Pankhurst and Freeman 2001: 335).

The new constitution of 1995 clearly banned discrimination against anyone based on social background. However, some authors claim that the situation of status groups has declined under the EPRDF (see, for example, Aalen 2011, Data 2012, Gezaghn 2003, Vaughan 2003), as the introduction of ethnic federalism has helped revive cultural values and local traditions, including ideas about occupational groups and slave descendants.[17] In the last twenty-five years, local authorities have been re-empowered and local hierarchies revived (Tronvoll and Hagmann 2012), while artisans and descendants of slaves 'continue to be excluded from the major arenas of social and political life' (Aalen 2011: 186). Moreover, with the downfall of the *Derg*, many of the privileges given to minorities were withdrawn, and some minorities groups were even forced to return land given to them under the land reform (Pankhurst and Freeman 2001: 336). As, according to Vaughan (2003: 277), prejudices are often shared by local administrators, civil servants, judges and police officers – who come from the locality in which they work – the structural disadvantage for minorities in some places is difficult to overcome.

To the outside, the integration of marginalized groups seems to have been achieved. But this makes it difficult for them to form a political movement and only a few examples of politically active minorities have been reported (see Yoshida 2013 on the Manjo in Kaffa). Besides, as Pankhurst and Freeman (2001: 336) state, 'since most of the marginalized minorities are dispersed social categories rather than localized ethnic groups, their concerns have hardly been considered in the new "ethnic" politics.' (see the example of the Mao and Komo, Meckelburg 2018).

While the recent literature emphasizes the revitalized marginalization of status groups under ethnic federalism, some positive changes have also been mentioned and deserve

17 Examples in the literature are Wolayta, where equal participation of all ethnic groups in national politics revived the marginalization of status groups (Aalen 2012); Dawro, where the result of the 2005 parliamentary elections was strongly influenced by the social status and clan membership of the candidates, rather than by their personal commitment (Data 2012); and Gamo where practices banned under the *Derg* were reinstituted after 1991 (Freeman 2004).

more research. The constitution of 1995 guaranteed the right to equal treatment for all citizens of Ethiopia (Article 25) and thereby provided the possibility of using legal process to achieve more equality. Yoshida (2013) has shown how the Manjo hunters in Kaffa used legal procedures to demand separate or proportional political representation after their tense relationship with the Kaffa majority erupted into violent conflict (see also Vaughan 2003: 276ff). After organizing themselves into an artisan's association and beginning to own land, the Sidama artisans (*hadicho*) created their own self-administered district (called Dara) in 1992–93 and formed their own political party in 2000 (Aalen 2011: 136–7).

It seems, however, that there are structural problems and a lack awareness of legal procedures that have so far prevented marginalized groups from claiming more rights in relation to dominant majorities.

Religious conversion

The introduction and spread of new religions has led to both more integration and more marginalization of marginalized groups.

As Pankhurst and Freeman (2001: 344–345) have explained, through their strict food prohibitions, the Ethiopian Orthodox Church seems to have enforced marginalization of non-members, as consumers of impure food are considered to be polluted. On the other hand, the Protestant Church – which started spreading intensively in the 1950s – strongly propagates the equality of all human beings and actively promotes the integration of minorities. The fact that it presses its members to abandon traditional beliefs and practices involves the breaking down of cultural and social barriers. Some improvement in the relationship between minority and majority has been mentioned in relation to Dawro (Data 1997) and Wolayta (Berhanu 2001). Samuel's (2016, 2018) in-depth study on the Dawro has shown that conversion to Evangelical Christianity softened the social differentiation between the *malla* (dominant famers) and the Manja (a despised group of former hunters) in certain areas of life, even if it has not been completely overcome and the extent of change varies greatly in different parts of Dawro. In Banna, conversion to Protestantism has led to a blurring of social boundaries, which allows intermarriage with members of other ethnic groups as well as with the special group of the *bajje*, whose males marry endogamously and whose females can only be married as co-wives in Banna, Hamar and Bashada (Epple 2005). Around Protestant churches, share-cropping arrangements between farmers and hunters/craftworkers can be found and social interaction has increased (Pankhurst and Freeman 2001: 346).[18]

In some places conversion has not led to integration at all. In Ganta, for example, separate Protestant churches had to be built for slave descendants because farmers refused to share the same church (Bosha 2018), and in the highlands of Amhara, slave descendants can be members of the Orthodox Church but are still not allowed to serve in the Church (Kiya 2018). In Oyda (Dereje 2001: 177), the fundamental difference between farmers and craftworkers is even justified locally by reference to the Bible, in

18 It should be noted that all the studies I found looked at conversion to Orthodox and Protestant Christianity. I could not find any studies on how conversion to Islam has influenced the position of status groups in Ethiopia.

which it is stated that craftworkers were descendants of Cain, while Abel was the forefather of the farmers.

Another negative effect of conversion to Christianity is the loss of craftworkers' and hunters' special powers, ritual offices and social roles, which effectively gave them some importance in society. The Waata (hippo hunters from Lake Zeway) (Gemeda 2016), for example, used to play significant roles among the Arsi-Oromo in the reconciliation of conflicts, the adoption of children and the inclusion of war captives or other strangers into the society. They performed fertility rites, protected the community and its animals against misfortune and disease, and were feared for their power to curse. For their services the Waata were highly respected and remunerated with food. After converting to Christianity, the Arsi-Oromo no longer needed the social and religious services of the Waata. The same was reported for the Manjo, who – having lost their ritual responsibilities among the dominant Kaffa – have not found an alternative way to gain influence or participation (Yoshida 2018).

Economic environment

The economic empowerment of craftworkers and slave descendants has changed their relationship with the dominant sections of a society in some places.

When the South was incorporated into the Ethiopian Empire in the late nineteenth century, the high number of northern soldiers stationed in the South increased demand for some craftworkers' products. As the soldiers had a great need for textiles, many craftworkers and even farmers (for example, among the Konso and Burji) turned to weaving, although they faced some resistance from the original weavers (Amborn 2018). Half a century later, as we have seen, when Emperor Haile Selassie prohibited the wearing of leather clothing, many tanners became blacksmiths or weavers (Amborn 1990: 59f).

When Amhara settlers introduced the plough to the South at the end of the nineteenth century, this led to increased demand for ironware and blacksmiths experienced an economic upgrade. When ironware was needed for road construction during the Italian occupation, even farmers tried to become blacksmiths. The introduction of money motivated Konso farmers to engage in craftwork as a side business, as beer and meat had to be paid for in cash (Kansite 2017). The increase in tourism in the last two decades has driven demand for locally made products and blacksmiths, potters and weavers have begun making high profits, which have increased their social recognition significantly (Belete 2012) and motivated farmers to undertake craftwork as well (Ellison 2006).

When Konso farmers join the *fuldo* – a powerful craftworkers' association – they need the *xaudas'* consent and to perform certain rituals (Ellison 2006: 668). However, they can return to their former identity, so that the transformation is not absolute. Yet, as Ellison argues, the shifting of identities and occupations contributes to the reworking of social categories in Konso.

Ganta slave descendants have garnered respect by significantly increasing their wealth through cash cropping of bananas, although they have not changed their identity (Bosha 2012, 2013). Social boundaries between the hippo-hunting Haro and the agropastoralist Bayso have begun to blur partly because both groups began working together successfully in a fishing cooperative (Epple and Braukmann 2018).

Yet, as Pankhurst and Freeman (2001: 341f) note, while wealth is not a guarantee of better social recognition, poverty seems to always contribute to marginalization and exclusion.

Social factors

Through contact with other culture, ideologies have also changed. Amborn (1990) has written that, before Menelik's conquest of the South, social differentiation between craftworkers and farmers was based on a strict division of labour and therefore complementary rather than hierarchical (Amborn 1990: 390f). Together with their religion (Orthodox Christianity) the Amhara invaders imported the stereotype of the 'impure artisan' who has the evil eye and is polluting and dangerous.

Others, like the Manjo hunters living with a Kafa majority, experienced equitable treatment under the Italian government and, as military conscripts, under the *Derg*. This experience positively influenced their self-image and motivated them to fight for equal rights (Yoshida 2018). The *fuga* craftworkers of the Kambata have reportedly had a similar experience (Wolde-Selassie 2001).

In the case of the Bayso and Haro people, a kind of general 'identification with modernity' has contributed to an overcoming of the boundaries between these two small groups. Both groups have converted to Orthodox or Protestant Christianity and strive to adapt to the nearby 'town's culture', which is reflected in their changing material culture (clothing, architecture and household utensils) and eating preferences (Epple and Braukmann 2018), as well as in a growing preference for speaking Amharic (Sava 2018). The positive reception of locally made products by tourists also seems to have contributed to a positive self-image, as a recent study among the Konso has shown (Belete 2012).[19]

The efforts of succeeding governments and various NGOs to improve status differences through developing better techniques for craftworking had not led to any convincing success by the turn of the century (Pankhurst and Freeman 2001: 355–358), although in-depth research on more recent developments is needed here. Likewise, I could not find any detailed studies on the impact of modern education. One can assume that, as education enables economic empowerment, it may at least have an indirect effect. However, whether and how cultural stereotypes and relationships between different categories of people have been changed still needs to be explored.

Summary and Suggestions for Future Research

I have shown that there are both external and internal factors and mechanisms that lead to more integration and an overcoming, softening or redefining of social boundaries between different hereditary status groups.

The most promising external factors, which also offer a level of sustainable change, seem to be related to the economic success of marginalized groups, which often results in an improved standard of living and – in many cases – better social recognition by the dominant sections of a society and better social standing. Where crafts have become an attractive

19 At the beginning of the millennium, the effects of tourism on the status of craftworkers and their products were not clearly visible (Pankhurst and Freeman 2001: 357–358).

alternative occupation for poor farmers, intermarriage between farmers and craftworkers, and even with slave descendants, has become possible.

Political intervention has had a strong influence in some areas, but has not always been sustainable. Providing opportunities that allow marginalized groups to improve their educational and economic circumstances seem to be benefitting an increasing number of individuals – especially in urban contexts – and might show greater success in time. The effects of enforced contact, cooperation and equal treatment, as well as the prohibition of discrimination often seem to be superficial and have only partially contributed to a blurring of social boundaries, if at all.

Contact with other ideologies locally has led to some changes in attitude and behaviour in the past and continues to do so today. However, awareness-raising programmes and knowledge about rights have so far encouraged only a few minorities to demand political participation, self-administration and equal treatment in the courts.

Religious conversion to Orthodox and Protestant Christianity has had different effects in different places. Generally, the dominant and often discriminatory behaviour of farmers towards certain hereditary status groups has diminished and social interactions become more sociable and cooperative. However, in some areas, converts to the same religion refuse to share the same church and different churches have had to be built for farmers, craftworkers and slaves. The effects of conversion to Islam have not yet been explored.

The success of internal efforts made by some marginalized groups depends greatly on their acceptance by the dominant sections of the society. Cultural, linguistic and religious adaptation to the majority have led to a partial merging of some marginalized and dominant groups, but integration has remained only superficial for others. Where a change in economic environment was met with local efforts to succeed economically, this has led to some successes. In a few places, status groups have deliberately emphasized their difference in order to achieve their goal of independence, while in others they have internalized their own marginalization to such an extent that it inhibits integration.

The above-mentioned arguments are based on existing research that is by no means exhaustive. Some data is scarce and not substantial enough to draw clear conclusions. Therefore, more research needs to be done to sustain the existing data and fill the gaps.

In my view, future studies must continue to follow Freeman and Pankhurst's suggestion and study the perspective of the marginalized status groups themselves. Although, the views of dominant majorities must also be included because no change can be achieved without their participation.

While contemporary research is focusing on challenges and difficulties, existing potential for change (both through internal mechanisms as well as external intervention) should not be ignored but rather studied and used as an asset.

The situation of craftworkers and hunters is being relatively well documented, other status groups – such as slave descendants, ethnic splinters and or special groups and clans – should be included in the research, as they share similar concerns and problems.

Regionally, most studies are focusing on the culturally very diverse South, but more research needs to be done in the northern, western and eastern parts of the country. Interdisciplinary research (for example, with gender studies, linguistics, political science, history) would provide additional perspectives on the lived experiences of hereditary status groups and how they negotiate their dynamic relationships with others.

I would recommend that the following topics be explored further:

1) *Culturally immanent mechanisms for status change.* Little has been done on this topic, and even less with specific focus. The results mentioned above could be used as a starting point for a new project that would consider culture as the source of and resource for, rather than as an obstacle to, change and more equality in Ethiopia. Bosha's study (2013, 2014, 2018), which shows how the legacy of slavery was successfully overcome by a directed application of the traditional *wozzo* ritual in Ganta, suggests that this could be a valuable approach. Through my own research, I have observed how, among the Bashada, the *bajje* people who are marginalized but also needed for their ritual expertise were at least partially integrated through the intervention of the local ritual leaders (Epple fieldnotes 1999).
2) *Differentiation of ideal and real behaviour.* Only Amborn (1990: 304) and Ellison (2006) have indicated, with their studies on the Konso, that there can be a great discrepancy between real and ideal behaviour towards craftworkers. Further research would help clarify if the same is true in other societies.
3) *Gender, marginalization and integration.* Few authors have touched the question of whether there are great differences in the marginalization of men and women of different status groups and whether attempts at integration have touched them differently.
4) *Sustainability of change.* Even though there are an increasing number of studies on the integration of status groups through external factors, the question of how sustainable they are still needs to be answered.
5) *Reasons for the lack of the use of legal measures by minorities.* Though the constitution grants equal treatment of all its citizens, few minorities have tried to explore and exploit legal options to reach their goals. Reasons for this could include a lack of knowledge, information or coordination, financial constraints, fear of negative percussions by the majorities or others.
6) *Unpredictable and diverging effects of religious conversion.* The effects of religious conversion differ greatly not only among different groups, but even within the some group, as Samuel (2018) has shown for the Manja among the Dawro, where it led to a softening of social boundaries in some, but not all, parts. Other factors that may play a role, such as the attitude and efforts of individual priests or other influential people, should be explored. Research on the effects of conversion to Islam should also be done.

References

AALEN, Lovise

2011 *The politics of ethnicity in Ethiopia: Actors, power and mobilization under ethnic federalism.* Leiden: Brill.

2012 'Revival of tradition? The power of clans and social strata in the Wolayta elections', in: Tobias Hagmann and Kjetil Tronvoll (eds.): *Contested power: Traditional authorities and multiparty elections in Ethiopia*, 111–135. Leiden: Brill.

AKALEWORK Mengesha

2014 'Roots and manifestations of marginalization: an exploration of socio- economic and political facets of minority group in Wolaitta Zone, southern Ethiopia', *Global Journal of Human Social Science* (C) 14(7): 28–35.

AMBAYE Ogato

2017 'A cursory reflection on the research of the Frobenius Institute on the Sidama people of Ethiopia, in: Sabine Dinslage and Sophia Thubauville (eds), *Seeking out wise old men. Six decades of Ethiopian Studies at the Frobenius Institute revisited*, 251–264. Berlin: Reimer.

AMBORN, Hermann

1990 *Differenzierung und Integration: Vergleichende Untersuchungen zu Spezialisten und Handwerkern in südäthiopischen Agrargesellschaften*. München: Trickster.

2009 'Mobility, knowledge and power: Craftsmen in the borderland', in: Günther Schlee and Elizabeth Watson (eds.), *Changing identifications and alliances in North-East Africa, Vol I. Ethiopia and Kenya*, 113–131. New York, Oxford: Berghahn.

2018 'Continuity and change in the relationships between artisans and farmers in southern Ethiopia', in: Susanne Epple (ed.), *The state of status groups in Ethiopia: Minorities between marginalization and integration*, 121–136. Berlin: Reimer.

ANEESA Kassam

2000 'When will we be people as well? Social identity and the politics of cultural performance: The case of the Waata Oromo of East and Northeast Africa', *Social Identities* 6 (2): 189–206.

ANEESA Kassam and Ali Balla BASHENA

2004 'Marginalization of the Waata Oromo hunter-gatherers of Kenya: Insider and outsider perspectives', *Africa* 74(2): 194–216.

BEHAILU Abebe and Dea DATA

2003 'Dawro', in: Dena Freeman and Alula Pankhurst (eds.): *Peripheral people: The excluded minorities of Ethiopia*, 105–131. Asmara: The Red Sea Press.

BELETE Dawit

2012 *The commoditization of culture: The effects of tourism on cultural heritages and the status of artisans in Fasha, Dokatu and Karat of Konso Woreda, southern Ethiopia.* M.A. Thesis, Addis Ababa University.

BERHANU Bibiso

2001 "Wolaita", in: *Peripheral People: The Excluded Minorities of Ethiopia*, eds. Dena Freeman and Alula Pankhurst, 205–222. Asmara: The Red Sea Press

BOSHA Bombe

2013 *Social exclusion and integration in Ganta (Gamo) of southwestern Ethiopia: A study of descent-based slaves.* M.A. thesis, Addis Ababa University, Department of Social Anthropology.

2014 'Reclaiming lost identity: Redemption of slave descendants among the Ganta', in: Susanne Epple (ed.), *Creating and crossing boundaries in Ethiopia. Dynamics of social relations*, 73–89. Münster: Lit.

2018 'Heritages of slavery heritages of slavery and status transformation: Evidence from Ganta, Gamo Highlands of southern Ethiopia', in: Susanne Epple (ed.), *The state of status groups in Ethiopia: Minorities between marginalization and integration*, 65–78. Berlin: Reimer.

BRAUKÄMPER, Ulrich

2014 *A history of the Hadiyya in southern Ethiopia*. Wiesbaden: Harrassowitz.

CERULLI, Enrico

1922 'The folk-literature of the Galla of southern Abyssinia', *Harvard African Studies* 3: 74–82.

DATA Dea

1997 *Rural livelihood and social stratification in Dawro, southern Ethiopia*. M.A. Thesis. Addis Ababa University.

2012 'Family connections: Inherited status and parliamentary elections in Dawro, Southern Ethiopia', in: Kjetil Tronvoll and Tobias Hagmann (eds.), *Contested power in Ethiopia. Traditional authorities and multi-party elections*, 89–110. Leiden, Boston: Brill.

2017 'Goldmine and minefield. A native anthropologist's review of Eike Haberland's culture historical research on Wolaita, Ethiopia', in: Sabine Dinslage and Sophia Thubauville (eds.), *Seeking out wise old men. Six decades of Ethiopian Studies at the Frobenius Institute revisited*, 237–249. Berlin: Reimer.

DEREJE Feyissa

2001 'Oyda', in: Dena Freeman and Alula Pankhurst (eds.), *Living on the edge: Marginalized minorities of craftworkers and hunters in southern Ethiopia*, 159–180. Addis Ababa: Addis Ababa University Press.

DESALEGN Amsalu

2018 'The social reproduction of marginalization among the Kumpal-Agaw of northwestern Ethiopia', in: Susanne Epple (ed.), *The state of status groups in Ethiopia: Minorities between marginalization and integration*, 139–156. Berlin: Reimer.

DONHAM, Don

1999 *Marxist modern: An ethnographic history of the Ethiopian revolution*. Berkeley: University of California Press.

ELLISON, James

2006 'Everyone can do as he wants: Economic liberalization and emergent forms of antipathy in Southern Ethiopia', *American Ethnologist* 33(4): 665–686.

EPPLE, Susanne

2005 'Missionary work and cultural change among the Bashada and Banna of southern Ethiopia. An emic perspective', in: Verena Böll et al (eds.), *Ethiopia and the Missions. Historical and anthropological insights*, 153–170. Münster: Lit.

2010 *The Bashada of southern Ethiopia. A study of age, gender and social discourse.* Berlin. Lit.

EPPLE, Susanne (ed.)

2018 *The state of status groups in Ethiopia: Minorities between marginalization and integration.* Berlin: Reimer.

EPPLE, Susanne and Fabienne BRAUKMANN

2018 'Overcoming layers of marginalization: The adaptive strategies of the Bayso and the Haro people of Lake Abaya', in: Susanne Epple (ed.), *The state of status groups in Ethiopia: Minorities between marginalization and integration*, 79–100. Berlin: Reimer.

FREEMAN, Dena

2004 *Initiating change in highland Ethiopia: Causes and consequences of cultural transformation.* Cambridge: Cambridge University Press.

FREEMAN, Dena and Alula PANKHURST

2001 *Living on the edge: Marginalized minorities of craft workers and hunters in southern Ethiopia.* Addis Ababa: Addis Ababa University Press.

GAMST, Frederick

1979 'Wayto ways: Change from hunting to peasant life', in: R. Hess (ed.), *Proceedings of the fifth International Conference of Ethiopian Studies*, 233–238. Chicago: University of Chicago.

GEMEDA Hunde Wordoffa

2016 *Documentation of the endangered cultural traits of the Waataa community: Chopha village in Focus.* PhD Thesis, Addis Ababa University.

GETACHEW Senishaw

2017 'The Gedeo. Adolf Ellegard Jensen's ethnographic perspective', in: Sabine Dinslage and Sophia Thubauville (eds.), *Seeking out wise old men. Six decades of Ethiopian Studies at the Frobenius Institute revisited*, 265–280. Berlin: Reimer.

GEZAGHN Petros

2003 *Differentiation and integration: Craft workers and Manjo in social stratification of Kaffa minorities of craft workers and hunters in southern Ethiopia.* M.A. Thesis. University of Bergen, Norway.

HABERLAND, Eike

1961 'Eisen und Schmiede in Nordostafrika. Beiträge zur Völkerforschung', in: Dietrich Drost und Wolfgang König (eds.), *Hans Damm zum 65. Geburtstag. Veröffentlichungen des Museums für Völkerkunde zu Leipzig* 1(1), 191–210.

1962 'Zum Problem der Jäger und besonderen Kasten in Nordost- und Ost-Afrika', *Paideuma* 8: 136–155.

1963 *Die Galla Süd-Äthiopiens.* Stuttgart: Kohlhammer.

1964 'König und Paria in Afrika', in: Eike Haberland, Meinhard Schuster and, Helmut Straube (eds.), *Festschrift für Ad. E. Jensen*,155–166. München: Renner.

1984 'Caste and hierarchy among the Dizi (Southwest Ethiopia)', in: Sven Rubenson (ed.), *Proceedings of the 7th International Conference of Ethiopian Studies, Lund 1982*, 447–450. Addis Ababa & East Lansing.

1992 'Sklaverei im alten Wolayta', *Jahrbuch des Museums für Völkerkunde zu Leipzig* 39: 157–173.

1993 *Hierarchie und Kaste: zur Geschichte und politischen Struktur der Dizi in Südwest-Äthiopien*. Stuttgart: Steiner.

HALLPIKE, Christopher, R.

1968 'The status of craftsmen among the Konso of South-West Ethiopia', *Africa* 38(3): 258–269.

1972 *The Konso of Ethiopia*. Oxford: Clarendon Press.

HOEHNE Markus V.

2014 'Continuities and changes regarding minorities in Somalia', *Ethnic and Racial Studies* 38(5): 792–807.

HUNTINGFORD, George Wynn Brereton

1955 *The Galla of Ethiopia: The kingdoms of Kafa and Janjero*. London: International African Institute.

JENSEN, Adolf Ellegard

1936 *Im Lande des Gada. Wanderungen zwischen Volkstrümmern Südabessiniens*. Stuttgart: Strecker & Schröder.

1959 (ed.) *Altvölker Süd-Äthiopiens*. Stuttgart: Kohlhammer.

KANSITE Gellebo

2017 'Social divisions and their gradual transformation among the Konso in Southern Ethiopia', in *Ethiopian Studies in Frankfurt Revisited*, eds. Sophia Thubauville and Sabine Dinslage, 109–124. Berlin: Reimer.

KIYA Gezahegne

2018 'Living on the margins in the Rayya Qobbo Highlands: Slave descendants in contemporary North Wollo Amhara Region', in: Susanne Epple (ed.), *The state of status groups in Ethiopia: Minorities between marginalization and integration*, 157–171. Berlin: Reimer.

LANGE, Werner Jürgen

1976 'Dialectics of divine kingship in the Kafa Highlands', Occasional Papers, No. 15. African Studies Center, UCLA.

1979/80 'Status and functions of Kafa bards in feudal Ethiopia', *Northeast African Studies* 1: 85–90.

LEIKOLA, Kirsi

2018 'Talking Manjo: Manipulating a social boundary through new linguistic resources', in: Susanne Epple (ed.), *The state of status groups in Ethiopia: Minorities between marginalization and integration*, 219–241. Berlin: Reimer.

MECKELBURG, Alexander

2015 'Slavery, emancipation and memory: Exploratory notes on Western Ethiopia', *International Journal of African Historical Studies* 48(2): 345–362.

2018 'Minority integration and citizenship expansion. Observations from the Mao and Komo groups in western Ethiopia', in: Susanne Epple (ed.), *The state of status groups in Ethiopia: Minorities between marginalization and integration*, 173–192. Berlin: Reimer.

OLMSTEAD, Judith

1973 'Agricultural land and social stratification in the Gamu Highland of Southern Ethiopia', in: Harold Marcus (ed.), *Proceedings of the first United States Conference on Ethiopian Studies*, 223–234. East Lansing: African Studies Center, Michigan State University.

PANKHURST, Alula

1999 '"Caste" in Africa: The evidence from South-Western Ethiopia reconsidered', *Africa: Journal of the International African Institute* 69(4): 485–509.

2001 'Introduction: Dimensions and conceptions of marginalization', in: Dena Freeman and Alula Pankhurst (eds.), *Living on the edge: Marginalized minorities of craft workers and hunters in Southern Ethiopia*, 1–23. Addis Ababa: Addis Ababa University Press.

PANKHURST, Alula and Dena FREEMAN

2001 'Conclusion II: Change and development: Lessons from the twentieth century', in: Dena Freeman and Alula Pankhurst (eds.), *Living on the edge: Marginalized minorities of craftworkers and hunters in Southern Ethiopia*, 331–375. Addis Ababa: Addis Ababa University Press.

PANKHURST, Richard

1961 'Status, division of labour and employment in nineteenth and twentieth century Ethiopia', *Ethnological Society Bulletin* II(1): 7–58.

PINTO, Ambrose

2001 'UN Conference against racism: Is caste race?', *Economic and Political Weekly* 30(36): 2817–2820.

2002 'Caste discrimination and UN', *Economic and Political Weekly* 37(39): 3988–3990.

QUIRIN, James

1979 'The process of caste formation in Ethiopia: A study of the Beta Israel (Felasha), 1270–1868', *The International Journal of African Historical Studies* 12(2): 235–258.

SAMUEL Tibebe

2016 *Conversion to evangelical Christianity and its implications on the stratified society of Dawro, Southern Ethiopia*. PhD Thesis. Addis Ababa University.

2018 'The chances and limitations of integration through conversion to evangelical Christianity. The case of the Manja in Dawro, southern Ethiopia', in: Susanne Epple (ed.), *The state of status groups in Ethiopia: Minorities between marginalization and integration*, 49–63. Berlin: Reimer.

SAVÀ, Graziano

2018 'Code-switching from Bayso and Haro to Amharic as a status-change strategy', in: Susanne Epple (ed.), *The state of status groups in Ethiopia: Minorities between marginalization and integration*, 101–119. Berlin: Reimer.

SCHULZ-WEIDNER, Willy

1959 'Die Schangama', in: Ad. E. Jensen (ed.), *Altvölker Südäthiopiens*, 107–166. Stuttgart: Kohlhammer.

SHACK, William

1966 *The Gurage. A people of the Ensete culture*. London, New York, Nairobi: Oxford University Press.

SMIDT, Wolbert

2010 'Slavery and politics', in: Siegbert Uhlig (ed.), *Encyclopedia Aethiopica, vol. 4*, 680–681. Wiesbaden: Harrassowitz.

STRAUBE, Helmut

1963 *Westkuschitische Völker Süd-Äthiopiens*. Stuttgart: Kohlhammer.

TECLEHAIMANOT Gebreselassie

2003 'The low-caste Fuga occupational group under the Italian administration in the Horn of Africa', *Northeast African Studies, New Series* 10(3): 33–44.

TODD, David, M.

1977 'Caste in Africa?', *Africa: Journal of the International African Institute* 47(4): 398–412.

TRONVOLL, Kjetil and Tobias HAGMANN (eds.)

2012 *Contested power in Ethiopia: Traditional authorities and multiparty elections*. Leiden: Brill Publisher.

VAUGHAN, Sarah

2003 *Ethnicity and power in Ethiopia*. PhD Dissertation, The University of Edinburgh.

WATSON, Elizabeth E.

2006 'Making a living in the postsocialist periphery: Struggles between farmers and traders in Konso', *Africa: Journal of the International African Institute* 76(1): 70–87.

WOLDE-SELASSIE Abbute

2001 'Kambata', in: Dena Freeman and Alula Pankhurst (eds.), *Living on the edge: Marginalized minorities of craft workers and hunters in Southern Ethiopia*, 61–72. Addis Ababa: Addis Ababa University Press.

YOSHIDA, Sayuri

2013 'The struggle against social discrimination: Petitions by the Manjo in the Kafa and Sheka Zones of Southwest Ethiopia', *Nilo-Ethiopian Studies* 18: 1–19.

2018 'From social differentiation to discrimination. Changes in the relationship between the Kafa and the Manjo of southwestern Ethiopia', in: Susanne Epple (ed.), *The state of status groups in Ethiopia: Minorities between marginalization and integration*, 193–217. Berlin: Reimer.

Webpages

http://asiadalitrightsforum.org/interventions.php, last accessed August 10, 2017.

http://kmgethiopia.org, last accessed August 10, 2017.

Unpublished manuscripts of the Frobenius Institute

Haberland EH70

Waakka

Contemporary Contexts of Memorial Emblems for Konso Heroes

KANSITE GELLEBO

Introduction

The following study concerns *waakka*, memorial statues for 'traditional' heroes among the Konso in southern Ethiopia. I aim to describe the symbolic meanings of *waakka* and explore the reasons why they are erected and the current challenges around the errection and preservation of *waakka*.

The Konso are one of the Eastern Cushitic-speaking groups in southern Ethiopia. The community is organized into nine exogamous clans. Within each clan there are several lineages. The position of the headship in a clan is always hereditary. Extended families can establish their own lineage after some generations (at least five or more). Both the head of the clan and lineage are called *poqalla*.[1]

Individuals differ in their status, which are either achieved or ascribed. *Xormmuma/ Dhiruma* (the Konso term for heroism) is a valued status among the Konso. Men have to be clan chiefs, outstanding hunters, killers of human adversaries, or economically and politically eminent in order to be considered as heroes. Killers may transfer their heroic status to their respective clan heads. Sometimes, killers can transfer their insignia to their clan chiefs (or lineage heads) and Amborn (2002) suggests that this mechanism shows that the act of killing is a social affair. According to Konso tradition, clan heads are not allowed to shed blood, except during sacrificial ceremonies. Thus, in order for a clan head to be a hero through killing, their fellow clan members must transfer their status to them. The hero is praised and honoured by his family and the community. After his death, he is rewarded with the erection of statues (*waakka*) with small stones, known as gravels, erected in front of them. The ultimate purpose of erecting statues and gravels is to praise heroes and their spectacular achievements in order to inspire younger generation to be heroes like their forefathers. In this, these statues build a bridge between past and present generations (Thubauville 2012).

Methods of Data Collection

This paper is based on ethnographic fieldwork conducted in multiple locations in the Konso area. Relevant data was gathered from both primary (first-hand data from knowledgeable individuals and direct observation of places where *waakka* are displayed) and secondary (second-hand data from literature written by different authors and photop-

1 *Poqalla* are heads of clan. They wear silver bracelets on their right wrist. All Konso people are descended from *poqalla* families. Below these clan heads are lineage *poqalla* who are descendants of clan *poqalla* and wear iron or brass bracelets. Any senior family can establish its own lineage. There are only nine clan heads while there are several lineage heads.

graphs captured by individuals) sources. Informants were purposefully recruited on the basis of their knowledge of the culture of *waakka*. The major applied methods included:

- Observation: Visiting locations where *waakka* are displayed.
- Key informant interviews: Individuals with extensive knowledge about Konso culture and *waakka* like owner families of *waakka*, clan leaders and elders were interviewed.
- Personal experiences: I am a native of the Konso community and my own first-hand experiences, observations and knowledge about *waakka* have been incorporated into the study. However, I have tried to place my own knowledge in the context of other data sources to try and avoid bias.
- Photography: Several *waakka* were photographed to capture the details of the statues.
- Consultation of archival materials: Some historic images were retrieved from the Frobenius Institute's photo archive.
- Referencing of academic and non-academic media: These secondary data sources were examined to provide historic and ethnographic background materials for the study of *waakka*.

The Meaning and Representation of *Waakka*

According to local explanations, the word *waakka* comes from *waa*, which means 'something', and *aaka*, which implies 'grandfather'. Hallpike (1972) noted that *waakka* denotes 'something of the grandfathers'. The name indicates that *waakka* can only be produced and erected for male elders of the community, who qualifies the local craiteria of heroism.

Waakka are wooden anthropomorphic statues erected on graves, near a pathway, on communal ground or at the entrance of a village to represent the total achievements of dead Konso heroes (Hallpike 1972, 2008; Cowen 1978; Amborn 2002; Otto 2004; Poissonnier 2009, 2014; Awoke 2010). They are carved from the wood of the juniper tree, which the Konso consider to be holy and which grow in the large forests owned by the clan chiefs (Poissonnier 2014). These forests are believed to be sacred and *waakka* can only be carved from the trees that grow there.

During their expeditions to southern Ethiopia, researchers from the Frobenious Institute (i.e., Jensen, Haberland and Straube) were fascinated by the cultural phenomenon of the erection of *waakka*, which they characterized as an important element of the 'meritorious complex' (*Verdienstwesen*). They identified the three main elements of the meritorous complex as follows: (1) arranging and sponsoring large feasts of merit; (2) killing a foe or large game; and (3) the erection of a monument by the man's descendants to memorilaize him after his death and as a confirmation of his high social status (Braukämper 2003; Poissonnier 2009). Thubauville (2012) has written that the team quickly realized that the statues were of importance for their theory and so documented them thoroughly.

In Konso the noteworthiness of a man is sometimes ascribed, but mostly achieved by doing something considered remarkable: being wealthy; killing a male adversary or dangerous wild animal; being clan chief; or being a great war leader (Hallpike 1972, 2008; Cowen 1978; Amborn 2002; Kimura 2004; Poissonnier 2009; Awoke 2010).

The erection of *waakka* follows large-scale memorial ceremonies[2] (Shako 2004; Thubauville 2012). The authorized wood carver – chosen for his skill – is invited to the house of the dead hero. While working on a *waakka*, the wood carver lives in the family's compound (Poissonnier 2014), where he receives payment for his work and is supplied with good food, including meat, honey and alcohol (Watson 1998). Before he arrives, *jaqa* – a local alcoholic beverage – is prepared, honey is made ready and a goat is butchered for him. Until he finishes carving the wooden sculptures, he consumes the meat and drinks the *jaqa* mixed with honey. The food and drink is offered daily on behalf of the deceased because it is believed that the carver is connected with the dead hero (Poissonnier 2014). It is a symbol of respecting and honoring the deceased. After finalizing his task, in addition to cash, the carver receives a big gourd of *jaqa*. As the payment is costly, families of the deceased order *waakka* according to their wealth and capacity.

On the day of the erection of a *waakka*, lineage members, neighbours, relatives and villagers (in the case of clan *poqalla*) are invited to attend the ceremony. Invitees may bring *jaqa* to the house of the hero. Poissonnier (2009, 2014) states that the larger the group of descendants, the greater the feast and the bigger and more expensive the monument. A ceremonial dance called *shileta*[3] is performed. During the erection, the statues are painted red with dye made from a kind of rocky soil (Shako 2004). Either a goat or an ox is slaughtered to accompany the ceremony and chyme and blood are placed on the grave of the hero.

Fig. 1: Author with a group of *waakka* in the public space of Debana village

2 For the clan chiefs the erection of *waakka* is carried out after nine years. The corpse of the chief is mummified and both the burial and the representation of *waakka* is made on the same day. For other heroes, the ceremony depends on the ability of the family to make all the necessary arrangements. But families always need at least a year to conduct the ceremony. The ceremony is a rite of passage conducted to incorporate the dead into the world of the dead.

3 *Shileta* is a mourning dance performed when a person dies after his/her son has given birth to a grandson. It is performed for elders of both sexes, even though they may not have *waakka*.

Waakka always face the road and stand in a straight line. They are usually erected on the family's or a lineage member's farmland situated near to a main road. As Poissonnier states: 'Only outstanding deceased people's monuments are allowed to be erected on a communal village ground and can be remembered as "more heroic" than others' (Poissonnier 2014). Such types of monument are very rare throughout Konso. For example, as you can see from figure 1, only individuals who have made extraordinary contribution to the village are represented in public spaces. The *waakka* of many heroes can be displayed together on the same row. If the graveyard is situated on the main road, *waakka* can be be erected close to the tomb. I found only one clan chief informant whose family's *waakka* are placed on the tomb.

Waakka always appear in groups (Amborn 2002) with the hero in the middle surrounded by his wife (wives), slain enemies, animals killed, weapons used and other achievements, for example, figures that symbolize the deceased person's farmland. Many authors have described the arrangement and characteristics of these figures (Hallpike 1972, 2008; Cowen 1978; Amborn 2002; Shako 2004; Poissonnier 2009; Awoke 2010; Jensen 1936 cited in Thubauville 2012; Richer 2016).

Symbolism is the major feature of *waakka* statues. Every statue has its own symbolic meaning. The tallest statue, usually with *xhallassha* (phallic forehead ornament) and a visible penis, represents the hero. It is skillfully curved, as are the spears, Konso shields and, more recently, Kalashnikov guns that surround him. Next to him in a line – again finely carved – stand his wives; the first one on the right and the second on the left side, both wearing traditional bead necklaces. Slain enemies are roughly carved, represented as thin and castrated and positioned on the extremes of the line. All *waakka* have eyes made from ostrich eggs. Black colour is applied to mark eyebrows. A game animal killed by the hero is shown in front of the statues, where one can also find gravels representing the number of agricultural fields he owned in his lifetime (Shako 2004).

Fig. 2: *Waakka* with Kalashnikov

Some *waakka* of *poqalla* contain wooden sticks with notches that represents the number of successive generations.

Challenges to the Continuation of the Tradition of *Waakka*

The construction and erection of *waakka* is currently declining due to several challenges. Today, there are many conservative Protestants in Konso who are against many cultural practices including the tradition of *waakka*, which they consider to be objects of idolatry. Amborn (2002) correctly refutes this and states that, although Konso people acknowledge and respect *waakka*, they are not cult-like images and people do not worship them. A possible reason for the Protestants' condemnation of *waakka* may be a dislike for the ceremonial rituals performed when the statues are erected.

Fig. 3: Sticks with notches in a *waakka* assembly

Another human factor is the illegal trafficking of the sculptures. *Waakka* have been stolen and illegally sold to tourists and even on the international art market (Watson 1998; Poissonnier 2009) because of their artistic value and popularity among foreign tourists and collectors (Grant 2006). I observed a shop in Addis Ababa where both inauthentic and real *waakka* were displayed for sale. The fake ones are sold for a cheap price but the real ones are expensive. Poissonnier (2009) has correctly stated that 'many of the older and more valuable sculptures have disappeared all together from the villages of the Konso and the administrative authorities of that region feared that they might soon disappear completely'. Moreover, even if stolen *waakka* are found and returned to the community, according to Konso culture, it is forbidden to re-erect them (Richer 2016). Since *waakka* erection is associated with burial, people believe that a person dies only once and cannot be buried twice. Therefore, families that have *waakkas* rescued from the black market and returned to them, hesitate to re-erect them.

The rapid expansion of modernity has also had an adverse impact on the *waakka* tradition. Today, the younger generation is indifferent to indigenous cultural practices in general and the customs of *waakka* in particular. Moreover, killing of enemies and wild game is forbidden by law today. As a result of the above explained factors, very few new *waakka* emblems are still erected.

All these factors mean that *waakka* are now very rare throughout Konso land. It is particularly difficult to find newly made, original *waakka*. Even though it is not culturally correct, some families have removed their own *waakka* from the original places they were erected and re-positioned them in or nearby their houses in order to protect them from thieves. During my visit to the villages of Buso and Purquta in September 2015, I observed three families who had displayed their *waakka* in front of their main gate. One of the clan chiefs (Bamalle) also displayed their *waakka* in their homestead.

Natural factors are also challenging the sustainability of *waakka* figures. Jensen observed that most of the time they are covered with a simple thatched roof that covers the whole group of figures and protects the monuments from weathering (Jensen 1936, cited in Thubauville 2012). However, these simple thatched roofs decompose easily, exposing the *waakka* to damage from the sun, rain, humidity and wind.

Fig. 4: *Waakka* inside the village of Buso

Fig. 5 and 6: Damaged roof over a *waakka* assembly

Attempts to Document and Preserve *Waakka*

As Amborn observed, anyone travelling through the Konso region could not fail to be impressed by the wooden sculptures displayed along the roadsides (Amborn 2002). The earliest published photograph of *waakka* was taken around 1915 by Hodson (Cowen 1978). Azaïs and Chambard (1931) introduced Konso to the scholarly and public world with fifteen excellent photographs of *waakka* (Shako 2004; Amborn 2002; Cowen 1978), while Jensen (1936) and Nowack (1954) wrote descriptions of Konso *waakka* (Cowen 1978). Later scholars who have described Konso *waakka* include Hallpike (1972, 2008), Metasebia (2001), Amborn (2002), and Poissonnier (2009).

The 1934–35, 1950–51 and 1954–55 Frobenius Institute expeditions to southern Ethiopia were, amongst other things, meant to document *waakka* (Amborn 2002). However, the expedition members also bought and smuggled *waakka* from the Konso as well as from the neighbouring Kusume area. Today these are kept in the Weltkulturen Museum in Frankfurt am Main, Germany (see Figures 8 and 9 in Thubauville 2012). Numerous pictures of *waakka* and the carving of the *waakka* assemblies that were collected for the Weltkulturen museum can be found in the photo archive at the Frobenius Institute (see, for example, Figures 7 and 8).

Fig. 7a and b: *Waakka* in the Weltkulturen Museum, Frankfurt am Main

Fig. 8: Carving *waakka*

Fig. 9: *Waakka* displayed at the expedition camp

Poissonnier (2009) explains that concern that old *waakka* were disappearing prompted a mission to study and inventory the sculptures, planned and carried out by the Ethiopian *Authority of Research and Conservation of Cultural Heritage* (ARCCH) in cooperation with the *Centre Français des Études Éthiopiennes* (CFEE). The process of documentation led to the establishment of the Konso community museum. The museum was inaugurated in 2009 with the purpose of preserving *waakka* that had been rescued from the black market. The museum was also established as a research centre. In 1996 Ethiopian customs officials seized 200

Fig.10: *Waakka* display inside Konso Museum

waakka, illegally trafficked and intended for the international art market. These were stored in the Konso department of culture for about a decade, and given to the community museum in 2009. As mentioned above, as it is unusual to re-erect stolen *waakka* at their original home, some of the seized *waakka* were displayed in the museum while others were stored in the museum.

Fig. 11: *Waaka* in the IES museum

Outside of the Konso district, *waakka* are displayed in the Institute of Ethiopian Studies (IES) Museum and the Ethiopian National Museum in Addis Ababa (see Figure 11).

The former political party of Konso,[4] the Konso People's Democratic Union (KPDU), included a *waakka* in its party emblem and promised to help the society to maintain and preserve the sculptures (Shako 2004). The head of the party was Shako Otto, who understood the value of preserving the peoples' heritage and was committed to working towards the conservation of *waakka*. In spite of being a medical doctor by profession, he has made a valuable contribution to the literature on Konso, publishing several articles on Konso culture (Otto 1994; 2004)

Ethiopia has had its own stamps since the last decade of the nineteenth century, and these have been important in highlighting the country's natural and cultural heritages. In 2002, designer Bogale Belachew designed a stamp series featuring *waakka* that was printed at Österreichische Staatsdruckerei, Austria (see Figure 12). These stamps were and are still used by the Ethiopian Postal Service and have played a significant role in familiarizing the world with Konso *waakka*.

Fig. 12: 'Stamp series' used by Ethiopian Postal Service, 2003

Some tour operators place *waakka* figures on their web pages, while local hotels in Konso town also have *waakka* monuments and wall paintings (see figures 13 and 14), purpose-made to attract tourists.

4 After the downfall of the military regime in 1991, Ethiopia has adopted an ethnic-based federal system of government. Konso was represented by its own party (KPDU) until it was dissolved in 1992, when a number of political parties formed a coalition (SEPDM, Southern Ethiopian Peoples Democratic Movement) representing fifty-six ethnic groups in the Southern Nations, Nationalities and Peoples Region.

Fig. 13: *Waakka* at Green Hotel

Fig. 14: A sketch of *waakka* at Konso Edget Hotel No.1

Fig. 15: Small *waakka* produced for sale to tourists

Fig. 16: Display of *waakka* at village gate and a communal house to show the leading generation's achievements

Some local craftsmen and children produce small *waakka* for sale to tourists travelling to/from South Omo (see Figure 15). There is no specific social category who produce these *waakka*, and any skilful person can carve them both for sale or for the dead hero. Most of the producers sell them to tourist guides – who sell them on to tourists – for little money and the work does not provide their primary income.

The *waakka* display at the main gate of Majjala village (see figure 16) is contributing to the preservation of the *waakka* tradition, albeit in a new form: they do not represent an individual hero but represent community achievement as a whole. This is a new invention that has never been seen before. Some of these new structures of *waakka* display the heroism of all the village men – the generation at power. The generation that rules the community is required to accomplish certain things – for example, building new or repairing old public places (*moora*) – and must be renowned for its leadership and management of the community's resources. Traditionally, after retiring, stones would have been erected in some places to commemorate its achievements.

The Future of *Waakka*

The *waakka* tradition is undoubtedly under threat as the depredations of theft, decay, youthful indifference, and outdatedness take their toll. Yet, these challenges are not insurmountable, and a determined effort to conserve and reinvigorate this valuable piece of Konso heritage could secure the *waakka*'s future.

In the first place, there is a need for periodic inventory and documentation work on the existing *waakka*. This would help to identify the status of the remaining *waakka* in the region. As Christians are against the tradition of *waakka*, continuous and unreserved attempts should be made to make the younger generations in Konso aware of the value of *waakka* in preserving their identity, culture and history. Also, the whole community should protect genuine *waakka* from theft and smuggling. Moreover, the *waakka* tradition could be continued and adapted for modern times. Traditional criteria for heroism – such as hunting and killing – for example, should be changed for criteria with contemporary value: success in business, good education, community service, serving in the military, etc. Finally, souvenir shops should be established in different places in order to provide inauthentic *waakka* for tourists.

References

AMBORN, Hermann

2002 'Concepts in wood and stone. Socio-religious monuments of the Konso of Southern Ethiopia', *Zeitschrift für Ethnologie* 127(1): 77–101.

AWOKE Amzaye

2010 *The 'heritagization' of Konso cultural landscape*. Dissertation in Partial Fulfilment of the Degree of Masters of Science in Social Anthropology, London School of Economics and Political Science.

AZAÏS, François B. and Roger CHAMBARD

1931 *Cinq Années de Recherches Archéologiques en Ethiopie*. Paris: Geuthner.

BRAUKÄMPER, Ulrich

2003 'The meritorious complex: A German approach to Ethiopian anthropology', in: Baye YIMAN et al. (eds.), *Ethiopian Studies at the end of the second millenium. Proceedings of the XIVth International Conference of Ethiopian Studies*, Vol. II, 706–24. Addis Ababa: Addis Ababa University.

COWEN, Chester R.

1978 'Wooden sculpture among the Konso and Gato of Southern Ethiopia', in: Robert L. HESS (ed.), *Proceedings of the 5th International Conference on Ethiopian Studies*, 217–232. Chicago.

GRANT, Christopher

2006 'Stones, slabs, and stelae: The origins and symbolism of contemporary Oromo burial practice and grave art.' *Independent Study Project (ISP) Collection*, Paper 263. http://digitalcollections.sit.edu/cgi/viewcontent.cgi?article=1260&context=isp_collection.

HALLPIKE, Christopher R.

1972 *The Konso of Ethiopia. A study of the values of an East Cushitic society*. Oxford: Clarendon Press.

2008 (Revised ed.) *The Konso of Ethiopia. A study of the values of an East Cushitic people*. Oxford: Clarendon Press.

JENSEN, Adolf Ellegard

1936 *Im Lande des Gada. Wanderungen zwischen Volkstrümmern Südabessiniens*. Strecker und Schröder: Stuttgart.

KIMURA, Birgitta K.

2004 *An archaeological investigation into the history and socio-political organization of Konso, South-western Ethiopia*. PhD Dissertation, University of Florida.

METASEBIA Bekele

2001 *Le Rôle des Pierres Dresséesdans la Société Konso (Éthiopie)*. Unpublished DEA, Université de Paris I.

NOWACK, Ernst

1954 'Land und Volk der Konso (Süd-Äthiopien)'. *Bonner Geographische Abhandlungen* 14.

OTTO, Shako

1994 'The nine clans of Konso', *Sociology Ethnology Bulletin* 1(3): 80-92.

2004 'Traditional Konso culture and the missionary impact', *Annales d'Ethiopie* 20: 149–180.

POISSONNIER, Nicole

2009 *Grabkult der Konso und kulturverwandter Ethnien in Süd-Äthiopien*. PhD Dissertation, Georg August University Göttingen.

2014 'Giving birth to an ancestor: Boundaries and brides between life and death among the Konso', in: Susanne EPPLE (ed.), *Creating and crossing boundaries in Ethiopia: Dynamics of social categorization and differentiation*, 147–161. Lit: Münster.

RICHER, Suzi

2016 *Death, bodily fluids and fertility: the Wakas of Konso*. Guest Blog Post, Phase 2: Anthropomorphic Wooden Figurines *https://thepallasboyvessel.wordpress.com/2016/12/06/death-bodily-fluids-and-fertility-the-wakas-of-konso/*

THUBAUVILLE, Sophia

2012 'Memorial for heroes', *Tribal Art* 64:84–91.

WATSON, Elizabeth E.

1998 *Ground truths: Land and power in Konso, Ethiopia*. PhD Dissertation, University of Cambridge.

List of illustrations

Women's Knowledge on the Move

How Maale Women Respond and Adapt to Contact with 'Outsiders'

Hanna Getachew

Introduction

This paper examines the historical factors that have brought social change and affected the experience of Maale women in Beneta (highland country of Maale). The Maale of southwestern Ethiopia have a history of contact with 'outsiders' – besides neighbouring ethnic groups – which started with the big game hunters of the late-nineteenth century. They were followed by Menelik's conquering troops and subsequent administrators and settlers, then the Italians with their bands of soldiers, successive administrators and policemen of the changing regimes, traders, missionaries and, more recently, the personnel of governmental and non-governmental organizations, such as health officers, veterinarians, literacy campaigners and school teachers.

Throughout this history of contact, Maale households have practised, and continue to practise, a time-tested form of agriculture and animal husbandry as their main means of survival. At the same time, Maale men and women have adopted new ideas and practices, learnt through contact with the 'outsiders' and which they have adapted in innovative ways to their traditional way of life.

This paper is grounded in the literature provided by the invaluable work of Donham Donald and Sophia Thubauville on the Maale.[1] However, it also incorporates life history interviews with individual women who were and still are part of the long social process; a vital source of data, missing from the works of Donald and Thubauville. The focus of the paper revolves around the following questions. How have historical and current external factors affected internal social relations and caused social change in Maale? What are the experiences of individuals around social change? How did the dynamic socio cultural environment guide the role of individuals in Maale? In order to answer the questions I have raised, we need to examine aspects of contact and interaction between Maale and outsiders and forms of cultural exchange in a historical perspective.

By looking at a sample of eight women's life histories, I will explore the ways in which Maale women have responded to contact with 'outsiders' and have creatively adapted and incorporated new ideas and practices into their own way of life. I will also consider how these women have defined and redefined their identity in relation to the 'outsiders' and in response to the various requirements of successive administrations.

Most of the sampled women involved in the research were living in Beneta at the time the interviews were carried out. The educational background of these women varied: two of them had attended formal education at primary and junior level; the re-

1 The author would also like to take the opportunity to thank Sophia Thubauville and Jean Lydall for their constructive comments through the write up process.

maining six had never been to school. Five of the sampled women were followers of Protestantism, while three of them were followers of their ancestors' customary religion.

Most of the primary data for this paper was collected during field research carried out over nine months (February to October) in 2011. The purpose of the field research was to gather information for a PhD Dissertation at the University of Messina, Italy, undertaken between 2011 and 2104. A combination of techniques, such as life history interviews, observation and the consultation of archival materials, were employed. The paper has also been supported by data collected during earlier field visits to Maale living between Beneta and Gongode. These earlier visits[1] to highland Maale, the frequent contact I had with my host family and the close relationships I built with them and other women informants gave me the 'freedom' of participation, allowing me to observe how Maale women deal with events that affect the everyday life of the community. The data provided by the narratives of women informants covers a long period of time, from 1935 to today.

The Maale People

The Maale have a heterogeneous myth of origin[2], as told by elderly informants:

> The two groups who lived in the Maale country before the Maale king and the present Maale people arrived were called Utili and Olasha. The Utili, who lived first, became extinct because of a big fight. Of the Olasha, who lived in the Maale country afterwards, nearly nobody survived an epidemic disease. As a result only two men, who survived from the Olasha, lived in the Maale country before the first Maale king arrived. These men were the Makana *godda* (chief of Makana) and a man called Are. They did not know how to make fire and just put their food into the sun to dry ...

Traditionally, the socio-political organization of the Maale places the *kati* (king) as the highest authority, with thirteen *godda* (chiefs) below him. The thirteen *godda* (chiefs) had up to four *gatta* (sub-chiefs) each, depending on the size of the chiefdom, to assist them. Today, official reports[3] estimate that 84,657 Maale live in the northeast part of South Omo Zone. They share borders with the Aari, the Hammer-Banna group in the southwest, and with Gofa people in the north (Hanna 2001). Since 2007 the Maale have had their own district (*woreda*) that consists of twelve villages (*gurda*).

The Maale are a patrilineal society with a patrilocal residential pattern. Polygamous marriages with extended family members are still common in the area, even though more than 50 per cent of the population has already converted to Protestantism, which only tolerates monogamous marriages (Hanna 2001; Hanna and Thubauville 2004). Although Christianity has spread widely since the 1960s, some Maale still adhere to their traditional beliefs, which are characterized by ancestor worship (Donham 1987).

---

1 Even though the formal data collection for my PhD dissertation was carried out over nine months in 2011, I had had the opportunity to a make a number of field visits to Maale since joining the South Omo Research Center in 2001/02.

2 Taken from a longer version of Maale oral history collected by the author and Thubauville (2004 and 2010) through intensive interviews made with elders.

3 This number was published in the last country-wide census, conducted in 2008 (Federal Democratic Republic of Ethiopia 2010).

The economy of Maale combines both agriculture and animal husbandry. While agriculture plays a more important part for the inhabitants of the mountainous areas, where coffee, papaya, mango and banana plants are common, the economy in the lowlands is defined by pastoralism and the production of maize, sorghum, finger-millet and teff. They also keep livestock, mainly goats, sheep and cattle.

A significant aspect of Maale social life is the way they work together. The work that individual households can perform is limited, so workgroups between households are formed to accomplish certain tasks much more efficiently. Working together is also one of the most important ways for Maale households to establish their identities. Who you work with says who you are and where you belong (Donham 1999).

As to linguistic classification, Azeb (2000) notes that *maalò mùcci* – *mallò* is the plural of the self-name of the people, *mùcci* means language – belongs to the Omotic language cluster found in the vicinity of the Great Omo River.

The Maale in Historical Context

The late-nineteenth-century campaign of conquest launched by the forces of Menelik of 'Shoa' was responsible for the creation of the modern Ethiopian state. It was during that time that the Maale and the remaining ethnic groups of today's South Omo Zone were brought under the Ethiopian state administration (Donham 1994; Tsega-ab 2005; Strecker 1976). The most important developments of the period were the establishment of Gofa-Bako as the provincial town in the South Omo highlands, and the subsequent foundation of the small garrison at Godda-Maale at the turn of the twentieth century. The selection of Bako, in the Aari highlands, by the forces of 'Ras' Wolde Giyorgis – who had been leading the campaign – was driven by socio-economic and ecological factors. As Tsega-ab (2005) puts it:

> Gofa-Bako's provincial rule over its subject peoples had marked variation along socio-economic, ecological and also to some extent ethnic lines. A glaring indication was the disparity evident in the highland areas of Gofa, Aari and Maale on one hand and the dominantly pastoralist areas of Banna, Mursi, Dime, Hamar, Bashada, Kara and Dassanetch on the other. As it can be seen in the name of the province, Gofa-Bako had firm control over highland areas of Gofa and Bako (which refers to Aari). Gofa, Ari and Maale are ecologically suitable to accommodate settlers of northern Ethiopian background.

Whatever the motives were, incorporation paved the way for another development in the area – the imposition of the *gabar* system.[4] The *gabar*[5] system was an administrative

4 The *gabar* system had been introduced in the South Omo region following Menelik's campaign of conquest at the turn of the twentieth century. In its true sense, however, the *gabar* system had been functional in the northern parts of the country well before the twentieth century. During this period, *rist* and *gult* were the mechanisms by which land could be inherited and tribute levied. While inheritance under the *rist* system depended on household and descent, in the *gult* system, loyalty and terms of service to rulers were what were expected of individuals. Following the decision of Emperor Menelik to offer *gult* grants to his officials, from 1910, highlanders who relied on cultivation for their livelihood were reduced to tributaries on their land. This is what happened to both Maale and Aari: both groups were turned into *gabars* who had to bear the responsibility of paying different dues.

5 *Gabar* means 'tribute-giver'. They were peasants who owned *rist* lands but were forced to pay tribute to gult holder (Donham 1987).

mechanism that lasted until the mid-1940s and brought drastic changes to the lives of the inhabitants of South Omo, especially Aari and Maale.

As is indicated in the quotation above, the selection of a provincial town on the basis of socio-economic and ecological concerns was repeated in sub-provinces like Maale and Aari. The provincial towns provided a steppingstone for the commencement of contact affecting the lives of the Maale who resided in highland areas, particularly in the northwest and west of the country. In 1910, all the western chiefdoms of Maale – Bio, Lemo, and Gento – were given as *gult*[6] grants to three of Menelik's officials, along with ten to twenty soldiers under them. In 1911, the governor of Bako established a second settlement of soldiers at Bunka, the heart of Maale. These events not only affected the ritual role of the Maale traditional king (*kati*), who later became a *balabat* under the tutelage of the Ethiopian administration, but also unsettled Maale families, who were supposed to render services to the insatiable settler soldiers.

Moreover, different sources indicate that inhabitants of South Omo's two highland countries, Aari and Maale, were enormously affected by the slave hunting that started soon after the campaign of the conquest. In this regard, oral history evidence from both areas reveals the extent to which Aari and Maale were affected differently by slave hunting, due to differences in the reactions of their traditional political leaders in that period (Tsega-ab 2005).

In early 1937, the invading Italian army seized important posts in South Omo. This was followed by the establishment of an Italian commissariat administration centred at Bako; the coming of Italian soldiers locally termed Somali or *banda* stationed at Bako (Aari); and the construction of roads connecting Gofa with Bako and Hamer-Koke (Strecker 1976; Tsega-ab 2005).

From 1941 to 1943, the southwestern province of the country faced a period of anarchy, following the evacuation of the Italian troops. The cause of the conflict is attributed to ex-resistance fighters seeking revenge on so-called collaborators (*banda*). In particular, revenge attacks and internal fighting were severe and rampant among the Maale, Aari and Amhara of Bako until late 1942. Among the groups of southwestern Ethiopia, the Maale, Aari (highland parts), Dassanatch, Nyangatom and Mursi (pastoralists) in Lower Omo were labelled as collaborators and subjected to revenge attacks by other groups supported by ex-resistance fighters.

Van Aswegen (2008) summarizes the most important events that affected the political and economic life of the Maale between 1941 and 1991. First, he mentions the abolition of the *gabar* system and the introduction of taxation in cash, based on a new system of land measurement called *qalad*.[7] The new system served as an administrative mechanism from the period of the restoration to the Ethiopian revolution (1941–1974). Further regulations were introduced whereby salaries were paid to administrative officials from Addis Ababa; the title of policeman was given to the former Menelik settler-soldiers; and government-owned land was sold to northern settlers. However, Bako continued to be a

6 A *gult* grant was permission to rule and dominate. This meant the right to collect money and services from peasants who lived on the land. This also included the right to production and *rist* (Donham 1986).

7 In this system of taxation, former *gabars*, such as Maale and Aari highlanders who depended on agriculture for their livelihoods, were required to measure their lands in *qalads* and divide it into three categories based on the degree of fertility – *lam*, *tef* and *lem-taf*.

provincial town and centre for education and medical services, as well as a major trading centre for the southwest.

On January 1954, Scandinavian and North American evangelists from the Sudan Interior Mission (SIM) – founder of the Kale Hiwot church – opened a mission station in Bako. During the 1960s, Christianity was spread in Maale by evangelists from the Wolaita – a neighbouring ethnic group – who had been working closely with SIM missionaries. The SIM missionaries stationed in Bako offered modern medicines and education in the Amharic language. The young men who attended Christian schools during the 1960s helped bring about the events of the revolution of 1974. This was because the education offered by the Kale Hiwot church at that time was underpinned by criticism of traditional values as 'backward' and support for the ideology of social change that helped the *Derg* to power. Under the socialist *Derg* regime, all rural land was nationalized and redistributed by peasant associations. Schools and clinics were expanded and university students from Addis Ababa were sent into the countryside as part of a major literacy campaign; they reached the Maale in 1975. All these events significantly affected their traditional lifestyle.

In 1991, the *Derg* regime fell and the Ethiopian People's Revolutionary Front (EPRDF) took power. The two immediate post-*Derg* events observed in Maale were the revival of Evangelical churches and the resurgence of earlier customs. The Maale, for example, were able to reinstall their traditional king (Donham 1999). Furthermore, an official report issued on 16 June 2008 by the Statistics and Population Office in Lemogento – a newly established *woreda* town – provides both statistics and details on the types of community development interventions that were being undertaken by both government and non-governmental organizations (NGOs) in every part of Maale. Among these interventions, health, education, economic activities, agriculture and social services received wide attention.

Recent interviews conducted with church leaders in Koybe (west Maale) have revealed that the numbers of Protestant church buildings and followers are increasing across Maale. The churches built in different areas of Maale are also important for the government's current aims for formal education, as they run literacy programmes so that followers will be able to read the Bible in their local language. These literacy centres opened by Protestant churches have created an environment conducive to both government and other NGOs' education initiatives in Maale. Here it is important to note that formal education began in the 1970s in Maale, with the establishment of the first school by Protestant missionaries. Yet the Amharic script had been in use before the opening of schools in Maale. In this respect, missionaries played an important role as they initiated the translation of the bible into local language and spread informal education in Maale by using the Amharic script (Thubauville 2012, 2013).

Life History Interviews

The following material from life history interviews provides an overview of the lived experiences of women informants and their childhood memories of the lives of their parents. The first part presents memories of people whom informants knew personally or about whom they were told by their families. The second part focuses on the direct life experiences of women informants from early childhood, girlhood to womanhood.

Reconstructed life experiences

Most of the informants interviewed were not alive during the brief period of Italian administration in Maale. Yet, they recalled what they were told by their families about that time. What looms large in their stories is the maltreatment they endured at the hands of the Italian soldiers. According to informants, Italian soldiers treated the men working at the road-building sites joining Maale to Aari and Goffa countries badly. Also, married and unmarried women were sexually abused by soldiers who visited the villages looking for more manpower and food supplies. The families visited by soldiers handed over what they had produced but were also expected to carry the goods to the road-building sites. The collected grains, honey and raw meat had to be transported by young or married men who were selected by the Italian soldiers. Men were assigned to transport food supplies and other materials from one road-building site to another; and women were required to serve the Italian soldiers by grinding grain. According to women interviewees, demands for labour and tribute during the Italian administration were similar to those of the *gabar* system.

The following stories from two women – Zelekech and Dikise – exemplify the shared experiences of the women. Zelekech recalls the experiences of her father at a young age as follows:

> I remember when my father was calling the name 'Atse' Menelik, I couldn't recall any of the stories he told about this period. But when I was little, our father used to tell us the story of the Italian period when all family members were sitting by the fire. He usually said 'Tsalian (Italians) brought us iron. We never used iron made tools before'. During his young age my father was taken by *banda* (Ethiopian soldiers who followed the Italians) to transport sacks filled with maize. My father walked the road from his village Koybe (west Maale) to Bako (Aari country). He carried grains at the road construction site in Bako and walked until Key-Afer (town located south west of the Maale). One day while he was travelling from Bako to Key-Afer he got very sick. His throat was sore that he couldn't swallow food and became very tired. He was left on top of the hill by the *banda* who continued their way ahead to Key-Afer. He recognized that the road was dug by many people, such as the Aari and the Gofa, who were not taken from Maale. He saw that the *banda* seriously controlled the work, and men who were exhausted due to the demanding labour were pushed down the hill at Bako. He observed women grinding and cooking. Our father told us that he spent a long time until he joined his family, who moved away from their *bao* (ancestral grave yard) again. Our father told us soon after he was taken by the soldiers, his mother took other family members and moved to Beneta. My grandmother didn't like the Italians; she used to call it the period which 'separates children from family'.

The other woman, Dikisi, shared with me what she had observed and how the situation after the Italians left had affected her life. As she put it:

> I grew up when the 'bow bow' sound from the airplane filled up the sky. Soon after, rumours like 'the *arbegnoche* (patriots or ex-resistance fighters) returned back from the bush' and 'the Somali have left Bako' were circulated widely among villagers. Then the Amhara who controlled Bako opened a war against the Maale.

> Many men went to fight the Amhara and we (the Maale) were able to chase them until Arba Minch. During this time my mother took all of us to a village near Boka (small river found in Beneta), our former village was on top of the hill and near to the war. We also fought with the Banni (common name for neighbouring pastoralists). The war with the Banni claimed many lives, including my mother's. After we had chased away the Amhara from our land we have been leading a peaceful life, there was no war and no sickness. Many new houses were built, the relative peace gave the families time to know their surroundings, including the forest, and farming plots were chosen. At this time, I remember I was a young girl and started to work with my age mates on the farming field.

From the above memories, we learn that different and gender-specific survival mechanisms were used during the Italian occupation, as well as during the three years after the Italian soldiers left the South Omo region. Tribute was paid in kind, and male family members worked as daily labourers. The payments they received were not sufficient to live, so the Maale fled their homes during Italian occupation. In particular, the flight from the western Maale lands was triggered by those living near to the road construction site. And the change in the place of residence was made by female family members, who shouldered responsibility for the survival of other family members. This shows that women had a significant role in creating a secure life between1937 and 1943.

So far we have heard about the survival strategies adopted by the Maale from the experiences related by just two women from our sample. However, the life histories narrated by Zelekech and Dikise were shared by the other women included in the study. In what follows, I will describe the shared life histories of these women from childhood – beginning just after Italian period – up to the present day, when interviews were conducted.

Lived Experiences of Women

Wodero (girlhood)

During the interviews on life before marriage, the women shared with me the kind of clothing they wore, the tasks they and their families used to carry out, and their memories of contacts with outsiders, including Amhara merchants and surrounding groups such as Aari and Banna. The traditional skirts and aprons worn by the women were of three kinds: the *shiro*, the *pido* and the *buddo*. The *shiro* – a skirt made from cotton strings – was worn by small girls around their waist and usually covered the front part. This kind of traditionally made cloth is still used by those who settled in the lowland area of Maale. The *pido* – made out of a small goat skin – provided additional cover at the back of the body, because the girls wearing it were old enough to do the grinding and it was taboo to show the rear of their bodies. The *buddo* – a leather skirt made out of five or six goat skins – was worn by young girls. In 2006/2007 *buddo* were being worn by girls in *Gongode* (lowland country of Maale), but I did not see any of the lowland girls wearing traditionally made *buddo* during my last field work visit, in 2013.

Understanding change through traditional costume

In what follows I will provide a description of traditional costume as recalled by my female informants.

The *shiro*

Small girls started to wear a shiro when they began to participate in simple daily tasks, such as taking care of younger siblings and following a flock of goats to nearby forests. Informants recall observing family members busy with preparation of clothing. This was one of the important tasks performed by family. A lack of the weaving tools needed to change the cotton into cloth meant that all family members had to lend a hand in the process of preparing cotton to be used either as blankets or clothing for small girls. Married women shared daily household chores, such as grinding, cooking, fetching water and collecting firewood. Both old women and male family members carried out other duties, namely caring for and educating small children, receiving visiting guests, and cleaning compounds. Moreover, the old men, if they were the *toidi* (eldest son), were responsible for making *kashi* (ceremonial rituals) for their families, and for their married younger brothers. The shared activities mentioned above all contributed to survival, and more tasks were observed by women informants relating to food production. Married men and young boys played a key role in food production by collecting special woods and sticks to be used to prepare bee hives, for digging and for the cattle kraal. Young girls played a role by weeding and working with their age mates to collect and carry harvests – mainly maize and sorghum into the granaries.

The *pido*

When the women first began wearing the *pido*, they were young girls who had begun to help their mothers with daily tasks, taking the opportunity to learn the skills embedded in daily duties, such as grinding, preparing carrying rope to tie on the calabashes used for fetching water, and other simple chores. They also began working on the farmland, watching over the crops to protect them from birds and other animals. Although most of the activities and division of tasks among family members were summarized similarly by my informants, they also recalled seeing male family members preparing the equipment used for ploughing with oxen at that time.

Moreover, according to most of my female informants, the *pido* phase was characterized by contact with 'outsiders', which left vivid memories. Shared stories of contact throughout the period when they wore the *pido* reveal three different forms of interaction with 'outsiders'. The first was with men wearing police uniform who came from the northwest, and who seized fire arms, snatched traditional weapons from the young boys herding cattle, and roughly punished male family members who were suspected of hiding firearms. The second was with outsiders who collected grain and/or honey. The third was with the *negade* (merchants) who came with their donkeys and were noticed in/around their villages.

Locally all these 'outsiders' were called *gali* – a person who smells, wears fabricated cloths, has a light-coloured face and carries firearms. And family members were able to use their wisdom and knowledge of local geography as protection mechanism. Hence, while the men gave in to the demands of the outsiders, the women ran and hid with their small children in the nearby forest.

The *buddo*

During this stage, young girls were expected to carry out activities they had learned and practised with their mothers in earlier stages: *shiro* and *pido*. It was at this stage that they learned newly introduced cooking recipes from their mothers. These were *wote* (a stew made out of beans and peas) and *injera* (a very light circular bread usually made out of *teff*). Most of them also learned the skills involved in the lengthy process of polishing the *mitade* (a plate made out of clay used for backing) bought from market. In addition, at this stage women learned how to prepare *samo* (a local dish made out of sorghum/ maize flour), bake *laddo* (bread made out ground sorghum/maize) and brew *alla* (a local beer made out of sorghum). Moreover, they used to weeding the fields and harvesting the grain and transporting it to the granaries. All the activities listed as being carried out by unmarried girls were generally referred to as 'working for fathers'. These traditionally assigned roles prepared young unmarried girls for the next steps in their life, without changing their identity. Soon they would be engaged in the process of *gocho* – mate selection by a pulling girl's hand in the evening – which eventually changed their identity from *wodero* (girl) to *lali* (woman).

Traditionally, the start of the period in which women wore *buddo* signified that they had already been engaged in farming activities. But for the women I interviewed, the phase during which they learnt the traditional tasks expected of a woman was interrupted when they were sent to elementary schools, which had been opened by the SIM (Sudan Interior Mission). The women went first to the schools opened in their villages to attend literacy classes (reading and writing alphabets in Amharic language) before moving to the elementary school found in Bako (Aari country).

However, even if they joined the elementary school they couldn't continue after grade five because they had no relatives with whom they could stay in the place where further schooling was available. By then too, they were old enough for marriage since all started schooling at a late age. Traditionally, unmarried girls were required to serve in farming activities, which were very important to their selection as a wife, before they went to their husband's house. But, by the time my female informants had reached marriageable age, the arrival of education in the area had changed forms of mate selection: young boys had started to prepare handwritten letters to communicate with the girl of their choice. The women in turn arranged their marriages either in the traditional way, where feasting and payment of bride wealth was minimal, or with a big feast and dressed in 'modern' clothes bought from the market.

During this period, family members were becoming more engaged in activities, such as the production of *teff*, butter, honey and coffee, that enabled them to trade for cash. Women were also preparing *injera* and *wote* to be carried by young girls and sold in the market. Thus the period witnessed ever-increasing forms of interaction with 'outsiders'. The initial and somewhat smaller from of exchange started in terms of spices such as salt has attracted women to take part in trading activity. During frequent visits from merchants buying *teff*, honey, butter and small domesticated animals – usually chickens – the female family members exchanged goods for coin. This form of interaction helped families to identify what crops and products were in high demand in the wider system of exchange. Honey and goats were also important in building *bella* – a bond friendship made through the exchange of goods – in this period. The traditional concept of *bella* was also applied by the Maale with the Amhara – the owners of their land – and the *negade*, which not only helped the latter, who could then leave heavy goods or spend the night with the family, but also enabled family members who moved more than previous time in the provincial town they could observe life, markets, attend legal matters in the court.

Experience of life during *lali* (womanhood)

The skills the women learned and observed from their families when they were younger played a significant role in sustaining their lives as adults and their families under the demands of succeeding periods.

During their early womanhood, most of the women worked in the peasant associations (PA) established in their villages. Some informants who had attended the SIM School in Bako had knowledge of writing and reading in Amharic language. Therefore, they were well-positioned to administer the women's associations organized under the peasant association. Besides participating in the peasant associations, the women sold *injera* and *teji* to the *zemachoche* (college students who came from outside). The cash they received from these activities not only covered their membership fees for the peasant association, which were 0.25 cents per women, but also enabled them to buy clothes and spices.

The women who had been taking goods to sell at far away markets, later on resolved the problem by developing new strategies. The community opened a market in their own village, Beneta, in the early 1980s. This market provided a good ground for exchanges with other villages and neighbouring groups, and even with 'outsiders' coming from the zonal town of Jinka.

My own observations of these women's daily lives revealed countless other activities they carried out.

Among those daily tasks are: attending programmes of prayer and Bible study organized in the Protestant churches in their villages; preparing meals and drinks, grains and vegetables that are sold at the Thursday market; interacting with other outsiders who live in the village by learning cooking recipes, hairdos, talking in Amharic language, sharing coffee, and making friends. In addition, women are recruited to teach their community at meetings organized by governmental and non-governmental organizations in their villages and at zonal/regional level. Most of the meetings focus on raising awareness of social issues, such as health (HIV/AIDS, malaria, family planning) and formal education, especially girls' education and gender issues. They are also involved in livelihood projects financed by NGOs that focus on farming, apiculture and credit services, from which women have emerged as immediate beneficiaries. Though some of them have been rewarded for their effort by getting the support of their children who have held important positions at the *woreda* or Zonal offices, most of the women informants are still investing in the schooling of their children. The women who send their daughters to school or college have to carry out the daily tasks alone and have to support their children in higher education by sending them the money they make selling meals, drinks and other things at the Thursday market.

Concluding Remarks

The life history interviews with women informants epitomize the survival mechanisms employed by individual families. The first part of the paper emphasized the role of women in dealing with change brought about by external forces in the past. By reconstructing life histories, an attempt was made to pinpoint how historical events – external factors and contact with 'outsiders' between 1937 and 1943 – affected the survival strategies of individual families and the coping strategies adopted by women. The second part examined the shared life histories of informants from their childhoods – right after the Italian period – to the present day. It was presented into two parts: the lived life of the women during their younger years, before they married, and their life experiences during their womanhood.

Above all, this paper had attempted to show that the life histories of women in Beneta (highland country of Maale) provide ample evidence of how external factors – land reforms, the opening of schools in Bako (Aari) and later in Maale villages, the establishment of associations, the arrival of *zemachoche* (students) in Maale, the introduction of policies on primary education, health, gender issues, the opening of offices at zonal and *woreda* levels, the emergence of Non-Governmental Organizations (NGOs) operating in livelihood improvement projects – and all forms of contact over a long period of time affected survival mechanisms in the past and continue to play a significant role in shaping the lives of the people in general, and women in particular.

The history of the eight individual women emphasizes the prevalence of social interaction between families who moved, seeking exile as a coping strategy, both from the Aari highlands (Bako and Shengama) and the central part of Maale (Boshkor, Asheker and Koybe) as far back as the 1930s. In this regard, exile or movement from one place to another looms large and appears to have been a crucial force behind today's mixed identity in Maale.

References

AZEB Amha

2000 *The Maale language*. Leiden (NWS): University of Leiden.

Central Statistical Agency

2010 *Summary and statistical report of the 2008 population and housing census*. Addis Ababa: Central Statistical Agency of Ethiopia.

DONHAM, Donald

1986 *The southern marches of imperial Ethiopia: Essay in social history and social anthropology*. Cambridge: Cambridge University Press.

1994 *Work and power in Maale, Ethiopia*. 2nd Ed. New York: Columbia University Press.

1999 *Marxist modern: An ethnographic history of the Ethiopian revolution*. Berkeley: University of California Press.

EPPLE, Susanne and Tina BRÜDERLIN

2007 *The pride and social worthiness of women in South Omo. The transcription of the intercultural women's workshop, held at the South Omo Research Center Jinka, Ethiopia, 4–8 Oct. 2002*. Mainz: Johannes Guttenberg University.

HANNA Getachew

2001 *Marriage and family system among the Maale people of Southern Ethiopia*. Unpublished B.A. Thesis. Addis Ababa: Addis Ababa University.

HANNA Getachew and Sophia THUBAUVILLE

2004 *Peace through Intermarriage: Interethnic marriages in Beneta, a Maale village on the border to Aari and Banna*. Unpublished Paper from a workshop at the South Omo Research Center in Jinka, 29 November–1 December 2004.

STRECKER, Ivo

1976 *Traditional life and prospects for socio-economic development in the Hamer administrative district of Southern Gamu Gofa*. Unpublished report to the relief and rehabilitation commission of the Provisional Military Government of Ethiopia, Addis Ababa.

THUBAUVILLE, Sophia

2004 *Maale material objects in their social and ritual context*. Mainz: University of Mainz.

2010 *Die Wandernde ist eine Kuh. Lebenweege von Frauen in Maale, Südäthiopien*. Köln: Köppe.

2012 'Brides behind bars: Maale women as captives between tradition and development'. *Paideuma* 58:213–228.

2013 'Local knowledge versus national development: Bride seclusion among the Maale as a period of preparation and consolidation'. *African Study Monographs*, Suppl. 46:97–120.

TSEGA-AB Kassa

2005 *An administrative history of Galab and Hamar Bako Awrajja (South Western Ethiopia)*. Unpublished M.A. Thesis, Addis Ababa University.

VAN ASWEGEN, Jacobus

2008 *Language maintenance and shift in Ethiopia: The case of Maale*. Unpublished M.A Thesis, University of South Africa.

Persistence of Polygamy among the Alle of Southern Ethiopia

BOSHA BOMBE and TEMECHEGN GUTU

In Ethiopia there are institutional, legal and policy provisions that discourage the practice of polygamy. For instance, the country's National Reproductive Health Strategy (2006–2015) states that polygamy, along with female genital cutting, early marriage and wife inheritance, is a principal social and institutional parameter that affects the Reproductive Health (RH) of women; and that success in improving the RH of all Ethiopian women hinges on the removal of these constraints (Federal Ministry of Health 2006). Furthermore, article 11 of the revised family code of Ethiopia (No.213/2000) prohibits bigamy. The Department of Women and Children's Affairs has been addressing these issues, teaching local women about their marital rights and encouraging them to appeal to the department whenever these rights are violated. Despite these efforts, however, polygyny is persistently practised among the Alle people.

This study aims at understanding the concept of marriage, emic explanations for polygamy, the situation of co-wives in polygamous households and changes in these practices among the Alle of southern Ethiopia.

Definitions of Polygamy

Polygamy is defined as marriage to more than one spouse at the same time. There are two varieties. The more common variant is polygyny, in which a man has more than one wife. The rare variant is polyandry, in which a woman has more than one husband (Shechtman 1980; Grey 2008; Kottak 2010; Nwazonobi 2013). In this paper we deal with polygyny, but we prefer to use the term polygamy because it is more commonly used in the literature.

The occurrence of polygamy has been explained in different ways. In the early days of anthropology, polygamy was believed to be typical for early stages of human social development (Engels 1942). Today, that perspective has shifted. Zeitzen (2008) argues that the existence of polygamy correlates with those economic and political systems where the most important resources are human resources.

Polygamy allows a man to have more children, providing him with a broader productive base, as he controls the labour of his wives and children to a large extent. On the other hand, Slomin-Nevow and Al-Krenawi (2006), working on the Middle East, associate polygamy with power and prestige. The larger the family unit, the greater its power, influence and honour among community members. A study conducted in western Africa (specifically Nigeria) shows that polygamy can be understood as a mechanism for building a security fence around one's life and family: it provides companions with whom to share thoughts and problems, and it supplies people who can help withstand attacks from other, larger families (Nwazonobi 2013).

Matz indicates that more than ten percent of all marriages are polygamous in Ethiopia; the rate is even higher in the Oromo Region, where approximately one third of married women are married to a man who has more than one wife. Polygamy is common among different ethnic groups in southern Ethiopia, including the Gedeo, Kambata, Gamo and Gurage, among whom it is associated with male prestige (Matz 2016).

Locating the Alle

The Alle are among the Cushitic peoples found in the Southern Nations, Nationalities and People Regional State (SNNPRS) of Ethiopia. They share a common boundary with several districts: in the north with Derashe, in the south with Borana, in the southeast with Konso, in the west with Bena-Tsemay, and in the northwest with Male, Kamba and Bonks.

The Alle are agro-pastoral people, and their livelihoods depend on the agro-ecology of their settlements: in the highlands, they produce barley, wheat and *enset*; in the lowlands, cotton and millet are the major crops.

Alle society is divided into two subgroups that are hierarchically ordered. Farmers hold the uppermost stratum and are called 'pure people or citizen' (*esako*). Subordinate to them are the craftworkers, who are divided into potters (*ore*) and tanners (*hadhe hasha*); both are considered impure, though the latter is considered the most tainted. As in many other Ethiopian societies, intermarriage between farmers and craftworkers is prohibited, and interaction limited and regulated (Freeman and Pankhurst 2001, Epple 2018).

This article is based on research carried out from January 2015 to November 2015 among the Alle of southern Ethiopia.[1] We utilized qualitative methods because it was important to understand some social phenomenon from the perspectives of those involved and to contextualize issues in their particular socio-cultural-political milieu (Glesne 1992). Data was collected from interviews and case studies with polygamous households (husbands, co-wives and children), local elders, and the Department of Women and Children's Affairs. Much of the data came from males because it was difficult to make direct contact with women; as a result, the descriptions below reflect the male point of view.

Concept of Marriage among the Alle

According to numerous interviews, the term 'marriage' (*akke*) has a double connotation among the Alle people. First, it implies an established bond between a husband and wife. The fundamental purpose of the union is to bear 'children', by which they only mean male children. This is because, according to Alle custom, every male individual is born with an innate debt[2] to his father. He is freed from this once he marries and substitutes himself by producing a son. According to local tradition, childless men and fathers of only girls have the same status; they are derogatively described as *bahako* (barren or one who has no heirs).

Second, marriage is understood as a tool with which to build up family/clan power. According to this perspective, marriage not only unifies couples but also integrates their respective families and clans. This view of marriage has a political dimension, indicating an alliance between exogamous groups. Such an alliance creates mutual benefits and

1 We conducted this research as part of our academic responsibilities, next to teaching and community service. We did the fieldwork on different phases and the project fund was covered by our university (Arba Minch University).

2 The duty to replace oneself and thereby ensure the continuity of one's family line.

joint responsibilities. Lineage groups that unite through marriage cooperate over social obligations, such as marriage ceremonies, birth, death and funeral rituals, and in times of chaos, especially during feuds with enemies. A large family/clan also contributes to social recognition and respect.

Traditionally, most marriages in Alle were arranged by the parents of the bride and the groom, a practice that is locally called *bottolungoo* (betrothal) marriage. The prospective spouses have no role in the marriage negotiations between the two families and simply accept their parents' decisions. Though boys sometimes suggest a potential mate, the final decision lies with the parents. Girls traditionally have no say in choosing their spouse.

Another form of marriage is made through the agreement of husband and wife, a practice that is locally called *marsee*. Both male and female informants explained that this form of marriage is less complex and, therefore, proceeds much quicker than *bottolungoo*. In addition, marriage payments in *marsee* marriages are less costly. It does not involve the parents endorsing the marriage. Instead, a boy presents his marriage proposal to a girl he likes through a close male and/or female friends or through his sisters. If the girl accepts the boy's request, they arrange a date for her to move to the home of one of his relatives.

Once she is there, the boy sends a go-between – usually an elder to his father – to negotiate with the girl's parents to accept him as a son-in-law. The marriage can only be finalized after all parties have agreed a process that involves lengthy negotiations and may take up to two or three months.

A third variation of marriage is through abduction, locally called *sitakko*. This is when a boy marries a girl by force. Among the Alle, this form of marriage occurs for a number of reasons. First, a boy may abduct a girl when he suspects or discovers that there is a rival man who might attempt to kidnap her; this happens particularly when they are already engaged. Second, a boy may kidnap a girl if her parents have refused to accept (due to some of the factors mentioned above) the formal marriage request made by his parents. Last, abduction may occur when a girl rejects a boy's marriage request. In short, participants (both male and female informants) substantiated that a boy abducts a girl when he fears that a planned marriage or elopement might fail.

Recently, there have been changes in the patterns and practices of two of the forms of marriage among the Alle. *Bottolungo*, traditionally the most common form of marriage, is now only partially arranged by the parents. Their involvement is now limited to checking the social background of their child's spouse and conducting the marriage ceremony. Mate selection, negotiation and decision-making are performed directly by the children themselves, or through their agents/friends. According to the participants, Christianity and its effects on indigenous culture are behind this change. Meanwhile, incidences of *sitakko* are declining because it is now a criminal offence and increasingly viewed with disapproval. These changes have allowed *marsee* to become the most preferred form of marriage today.

Through marriage, a woman is integrated into her husband's clan and she is called *kafikkoo*.[3] This means that, in everyday life, her husband's family members have the right to oversee her. When a husband dies, depending on the decision of his clan head, his brother or close kin inherits his wife. They are then socially and culturally recognized as partners, but their children are named after the deceased husband not their biological fa-

3 Meaning she belongs to all and is bone and flesh of them.

ther, because the purpose of the marriage is to ensure the descent continuity of the dead. In addition, the woman and her children continue to live in their own homestead, freely using the property; her brother-in-law acts as household head but only visit her infrequently.

Divorce is generally outlawed according to the local custom, even when issues such as barrenness, domestic violence, disagreements and conflict are causing marital problems. Occasionally, however, a husband may divorce his wife if he has the approval of the clan chief. In such cases, the husband has the right to remarry but the wife does not. If the woman wants to escape the situation, she has to leave the Alle lands and live in another community, where she might be able to remarry. Even then her new husband is obliged to pay compensation (*maaso*).[4]

Local Explanations of Polygamy

Among the Alle people, polygamy is fundamentally embedded in their perspective on marriage. However, we can classify the influences on the practice of polygamy into two categories: basic justifications (changing social status, patrilineality and male preference, levirate marriage, rite of passage to customary politico-religious leadership); and supporting (social prestige, social prohibition) factors.

Changing social status

Among the Alle, individuals who belong to a large family are socially respected in everyday life, whereas those from small families are less honoured and are marginalized. They are harassed in the drinking houses, market places and public streets. They may work with individuals from large clans in reciprocal labour organizations, but people reject them, claiming they can make no difference because they are inferior. They are sometimes even intimidated and their property (land and cattle) forcefully taken by men from large clans. In order to escape their status as vulnerable, many become involved in polygamous marriages, by which they can increase their family size, especially by producing to male children. The case described below clearly illustrates this.

> Case 1: Getachew was one of our key informants. His father bore nine children, eight were female and one was male. His father was rich and owned many hectares of land and cattle. However, he was single and unprotected and people disrespected him in the social arena. Repeatedly he was intimidated and harassed, his cattle were forcefully taken. Getachew grew up witnessing his father's troubles and chose to marry two wives, who bore twenty-three children (twenty-two male and one female). The first three children on their part got married and bore twenty-three male children. Others are on the way to that. Getachew said, including his grandchildren, there are forty-five males in his family and they are now secure and publicly accepted in comparison to the former shameful times.

Patrilineality and male preference

The Alle are a patrilineal society, descent is reckoned only through the male line and women belong to the lineages of their husbands once they are married. Because of this,

4 Compensation can amount to between 7000 and 8000 ETB in addition to cattle gifts to the ex-husband.

preference for sons begins at birth. Females are not as valued as males and are not entitled to inherit their parents' property. Some of our key informants explained that they became involved in polygamy because they had fathered only female children and worried about the continuation of their descent line.

Levirate marriage

According to Alle custom, when a woman gets married to a man, she totally integrates into his family. A family or clan head has social obligations to secure the widow's inheritance and ensure the descent continuity of their dead relative. This leads to levirate marriage, which prevents the widow marrying someone outside the family and the property of her deceased husband thus falling to another family.

Occasionally women support levirate marriage in order to preserve social acceptance. During our fieldwork, the Alle Woreda's Department for Women and Children told us that a woman had come to their office to complain that her brother-in-law had refused to inherit her for the fifteen years since the death of her husband. According to the Department, the woman explained that she had been waiting him all those years in order to maintain her social acceptance in the community, because divorce despises the status of a woman.

Among the Alle people, a younger brother has an obligation to care for and have sexual intercourse with the wife of his elder brother if he is absent for a long time, for example, when he is doing military service or in prison. In such cases, the levirate marriage is sustained until the husband is released from service or jail. On his return, the woman and any children born in levirate are given to him. The following case illustrates this norm.

> Case 2: Teshome was one of our key informants. He had been in military service during the military regime. During his 10 years in military service, his younger brother inherited his wife, who gave birth to a son. Upon the fall of the military regime, Teshome returned home with a new, Eritrean, wife. On his arrival, his brother returned his former wife and the son to him. Teshome explained that his brother did so with compassion, so that he would have many children. And he was happy with his brother's action. Nevertheless, his Eritrean wife had a culture shock, which lasted until she got socialized to Alle custom.

Rite of Passage to customary political-religious leadership

Alle tradition obligates the customary political leaders (clan leaders) to marry multiple wives. A clan leader may have married one or more wives before taking his clanship position, but he has to marry another woman, 'a crown wife', as a mandatory rite of passage to clan leadership. The crown wife is recommended and selected by the community members of his jurisdiction. She is selected from a pure and respected family and is considered the senior wife; all the wives before her are junior. Our informants confirmed that there are nine clan leaders in Alle, and each has more than five wives, an indication of their status and prestige.

Social prestige

Informants elucidate that 'affluent' men usually get married to many wives because they want to celebrate their status by having multiple wives. This desire for social prestige even encourages competition among women. Both male and female participants indicated that some women encourage their husbands to get married to other wives by saying, 'You are not less than someone, get married and let us have many children and be influential!' Such women arrange second marriages for their husbands and even share their household properties with co-wives.[5]

Social prohibition

According to Alle custom, parents are prohibited from having sexual intercourse once their first son gets married, regardless of their age and sexual needs. The restriction applies particularly to the woman; the man is free to marry another wife. Elderly informants elucidate that the prohibition is associated with the community's belief that violation of the custom causes misfortune and plague to fall on family members, cattle, production and productivity.

Polygamy and the Situation of Co-Wives

Alle custom prohibits co-wives from living in a single home. Polygamous husbands construct separate houses for each wife, in order to reduce distrust, suspicion, envy and conflict between them. Female informants indicated that, despite this, the relationship between co-wives is often characterized by disagreement and open conflict because of the unequal treatment they receive from their husband.

Polygamy causes unfair treatment of co-wives. Data collected from women who are married to polygamous men, local elders and key informants indicates that husbands often neglect their junior wives. This manifests in a lack of both material and emotional support. In Alle society, land is the basic economic asset, and when a man gets married to a second wife, he shares her piece of land so that she can grow her own food and manage her life. Thereafter, he is not concerned for her and her children. He does not visit them regularly and lives with his first wife.

The unequal treatment of co-wives is embedded in Alle custom. According to Alle tradition, the first wife is called *yaye dhammo* (first/senior wife)[6] and all others are collectively called *yaye lammo* (second/junior wife). Hence, it is customary for a husband to live with *yaye dhammo* and give her a special place. She is cared for and supported in every area of life; her husband extends both moral and material support to her. *Yaye dhammo* controls all the household assets: land, cattle and other basic properties. She also enjoys a privileged status in the public sphere. In the community, she is respected as first wife. Junior wives also respect the high status of *yaye dhammo* because the local custom obligates them to do so.

Today, however, the situation of co-wives is changing. According to informants, some men are detaching themselves from existing custom and living according to their own order of preference. One factor influencing this change is a woman's appearance. When a woman is lovely and beautiful, her husband usually clings to her, whatever her rank. Such women enjoy both emotional and material support at the expense of the other wives. The age of a woman also influences her position these days. During fieldwork, we

5 Recently, female competition is believed to have caused the expansion of polygamy among the Alle.

6 For clan chiefs only the publically selected woman is the legitimate senior wife.

observed that some husbands adhered more to young wives than to the older ones. In such cases, senior wives are left behind and are sometimes overlooked and undermined by junior wives.

The following case clearly illustrates the recent change in the treatment of women among polygamous household.

> Case 3: Ayelech is *yaye dhammo*. She said even though she is the first wife, her husband does not love and support her. He is not concerned for her and their children. He lives with the second wife. Ayelech said he discriminates and harasses her, saying she is old and his later wife is young and beautiful.

The emerging change in the treatment of co-wives causes jealousy and animosity between senior and junior wives. They often quarrel with each other, and are sometimes involved in open conflict. Some junior wives divert the attention of their husbands, but such actions further aggravate competition and conflict between the wives. One woman whose husband's attention has shifted to a junior wife said, 'man is softy seeker and he lives for his stomach i.e. he leaves one and clings to other'.

Changing Patterns in the Practice of Polygamy

Among the Alle, polygamy is still widely practised. However, subtle changes are being observed, which are being brought about by legal and institutional measures, the expansion of Christianity and the spread of modern education.

Legal and institutional measures

Data collected from Alle Woreda's Department of Women and Children's Affairs indicates that the government has been trying to implement the legal and institutional provisions mentioned at the beginning of this paper since the establishment of Alle as a self-administrative woreda. The Department has begun raising awareness of gender equality and the basic rights of women provided in Ethiopia's revised family code. The Department has also condemned polygamy as a harmful custom, and women are encouraged to appeal to the office when their rights are violated. Many literate women appreciate the legal provision and some have even brought charges against their husband after they married other women or are in the process of doing so. In short, women have begun to reject male domination and the asymmetric power relations they have experienced for so long in the community.

Nevertheless, in practice the rights of woman are not maintained. Women are still under male domination because of the deep-rooted custom of polygamy in the community. According to Mariam Mamo, an educated Alle woman who at one time worked as professional in the Department of Women and Children's Affairs in Alle Woreda, there are two basic reasons that stop the Department from working effectively on the issues under discussion. The first is that, unlike women, male members of the community do not accept the legal provisions made for women because they believe that they are against their very custom. Second, the justice bodies and courts do not properly address the appeals women make to them. Regarding this, Mariam said that the justice body tries to solve the problems of women by using a 'double standard'. For example, if a woman accuses her husband because of his involvement in another marriage, the court will not take legal measures, especially if his new wife has already given birth to a child. Often, with regard to the rights of the children, the court mediates between the two partners.

On the other hand, if a woman accuses her husband early – i.e. before his new wife gives birth to a child – the court punishes the husband and his second wife, sending them to prison for an average of eight months. However, when they are released from jail, the man often abandons his first wife because she accused him of involving in another marriage and then makes a life with the junior wife. The first wife and her children are ignored, not cared for or supported. In the meantime, the family of his second wife asks him for the bride price and this further damage the family's economy (the property owned by the man and his first wife). For example, Mariam explained that her brother married another woman and sold the land and other properties owned by him and his first wife to pay his new wife's family a bride price of 18,000 ETB.

The expansion of Christianity

In the 1950s Orthodox Christianity was introduced to Alle society. Today, there are about seven Orthodox churches. According to older informants, Orthodox Christianity has not discouraged the local customs and practices and, in fact, it exists in conformity with their customs. Orthodox clergymen and priests did not condemn and override the practice of polygamy.

Protestants (Mekane Yesus and Ethiopian Kale Hewot Church), on the other hand, have been radical in their approach, promoting monogamy as divinely ordered marriage and condemning polygamy. Polygamous men who embrace Protestantism are thought to divorce their junior wives and retain only their senior one. An evangelist from Kale Hewot Church indicated that young Protestants were more inclined towards the new order of life than toward the local customs. In addition, those who marry in a Protestant church live in accordance with the new religion's precepts.

Thus, the Protestants have achieved some changes to the practice of polygamy. However, the Church has been unable to make further transformations. According to Protestant informants, there are several reasons for this. First, many converts were already polygamous (having two or more wives) when they embraced the new religion and did not want to divorce their junior wives; they do not consider marrying extra wives adulterous, as the Protestants teach, but as a normal way of life. Second, some married Protestants who were involved in another marriage left the Church and returned to their former lives when faced with the Church's condemnation. Third, issues such as whether polygamous men can be baptised, making them full members of the Church, involved in the Lord's Supper and allowed to become ministers and leaders, became and remain a matter of conflict and disagreement among leaders and members of the Protestant Church. Finally, more than anything, the involvement of some leaders in polygamy weakened the Church's impact on the local culture. The following case clearly illustrates the situation.

> Case 4: Antisa together with his wife and their four male children live in Kolango, administrative centre of Alle *Woreda*. They have been member of Mekane Yesus Church for many years, and Antisa serves in the church in leadership and in other departments too. He is a well-known and respected person. However, he wanted

> to marry another woman and always insists his wife by claiming that he wanted female children. In the end he married the woman, and for the time being the church excluded him from the leadership, and later he was returned to his position. Today they (he and his wives) are serving in the church.

Participants had different perspectives on the case. Those from Protestant churches, especially monogamous men, argued that this man shamed the Church and its role in the community. Non-Protestants, on the other hand, claimed that it was right to marry other women and have as many children as possible. But the case clearly shows that local custom is more powerful than the imposed religion among the study community.

Modern education

According to the data obtained from Alle Woreda's Education Office, modern education is rapidly expanding among the Alle. Before Alle became a self-administrative district in 2011, when its lands were divided between Derashe and Konso special districts, there were only ten schools. Today, there are fifteen elementary and junior schools, one high school and one preparatory school. In the curricula of various subjects, polygamy is labelled as a harmful tradition, and consequently younger generations have begun to overlook the local custom.[7] However, during fieldwork, we came across some educated men – educated to degree and diploma levels – involved in polygamy; their attitude towards the local custom has not been transformed.

Conclusion

Among the Alle, marriage is understood as a reproductive strategy and a tool for creating social bonds. The study has shown that the reasons for polygamy are fundamentally embedded in the essence of marriage. However, the explanations presented are more male-biased and the role of women in polygamy is less represented.

Today, some changes have been observed in the various forms of marriage seen in Alle. While traditionally *bottolungo* was the most common form of marriage, today *marsee* is preferred. Similarly, certain transformations in the situation of co-wives in polygamous households have been observed. Although local custom acknowledges that the first wife is senior and that husbands should live with them, in practice, some men have detached themselves from tradition and begun to live according to their choice and order of preference.

The changes to the practice of polygamy, on the other hand, are subtle. Despite legal and institutional provisions, the expansion of Christianity and the growth of modern education, polygamy is persistently practised. This persistence is surely related to the benefit the Alle community obtains from polygamy. As Grey concluded some years ago:

> The logical conclusion must be that the incentives for polygyny retain considerable vigour even in contemporary sub-Saharan Africa, so that the institution perseveres in the face of rapid, ostensibly antipathetic, socio-economic change' (Grey 2008:7).

7 A fourth grade student from Kolango said that, 'it is better to be orphan than to grow up in a polygamous household'. His father has three wives and he was born from the third wife. The student explains that his siblings and their mother are not cared for, they are marginalized and ignored. The entire burden rests on their mother. Considering all this, he claims that polygamy is a bad custom.

References

ENGELS, Friedrich

1942 *The origins of family, private property, and the state*. New York: International Publishers.

EPPLE, Susanne

2018 'The transformation of status groups in Ethiopia: Recent observation', in: Susanne EPPLE (ed.), *The state of status groups in Ethiopia: Minorities between marginalization and integration*, 33–48. Reimer: Berlin.

FEDERAL DEMOCRATIC REPUBLIC of ETHIOPIA

1995 *Constitution of the Federal Democratic Republic of Ethiopia (FDRE)*. Addis Ababa, Ethiopia.

2000 *The revised family law*. Addis Ababa, Ethiopia.

FEDERAL MINISTRY OF HEALTH (MOH)

2006 *The national reproductive health strategy (2006–2015)*. Addis Ababa, Ethiopia.

FREEMAN, Dena and Alula PANKHURST (eds.)

2001 *Living on the edge: Marginalized minorities of craft workers and hunters in Southern Ethiopia*. Addis Ababa: Addis Ababa University Press.

GLESNE, Corrine

1992 *Becoming qualitative researchers*. Boston and New York: Pearson Education Inc.

GREY, Sam

2008 'Polygamy: Historical rights and contemporary relevance: Explaining the persistence of polygamy in Sub-Saharan Africa', *Undercurrent Journal* 5(3): 6–18.

KOTTAK, Conrad P.

2010 *Mirror for humanity: A concise introduction to cultural anthropology* (7th Edition). New York: McGraw-Hill Publisher.

MATZ, Julia Anna

2016 'Productivity, rank and returns in polygamy', *Demography* 53(5): 1319–1350.

NWAZONOBI, Ebere P.

2013 'Polygamy in dialogue with ethics: A case study of Isiala- Mbano local government area of Imo State, Nigeria', *Ilorin Journal of Religious Studies* 3(2): 117–132.

SHECHTMAN, Amyra

1980 'The economics of polygamy', *Research in Population Economics* 2: 321–350.

SLOMIN-NEVOW, Vered and Alean AL-KRENAWI

2006 Success and failure among polygamous families: The experience of wives, husbands, and children', *Family Process* 45(3): 273–389.

ZEITZEN, Miriam K.

2008 *Polygamy: A cross-cultural analysis*. New York: Berg Publisher

Border Narratives and Ethnogenesis along the Southwestern Ethiopian Frontier

The Experience of Nyangatom

ELIAS ALEMU

Introduction

This paper explores the coping strategies adopted by Nyangatom communities situated along the crossroads of Ethiopia, Kenya and South Sudan. Ever since their incorporation into the Ethiopian state in the late nineteenth century, the Nyangatom – a small agro-pastoral group – have come into contact with a host of outsiders, including travellers, tourists, missionaries, pastoral neighbours and government representatives of the various Ethiopian regimes and bordering states. For the last four decades, the Nyangatom have been affected by the overlapping wars of the three states that influence the area in which they live. Nyangatom communities have been exposed to massive infiltration by machine guns, which has led to more frequent and widespread conflicts with neighbouring ethnic groups across the pastoralist continuum of southern Ethiopia, northern Kenya and South Sudan. The following article attempts to examine the patterns of interaction that evolved over time among Nyangatom, their pastoral neighbours and the surrounding states along the border.

Borders and boundaries have long been the focus of academic inquiry. Yet, like many other issues in the field of social science, boundary/border studies suffer from a lack of adequate theorization. Concepts such as border, boundary and frontier are often used haphazardly and possess overlapping meanings. Widely differing conceptualizations of the limits of social groups have also made academic discussion on borders inconsistent (Baud and van Schendel 1997; Rankin and Schofield 2004). A survey of the literature shows three major approaches in the study of borders: (1) borders as activities, processes and discourses; (2) borders as a means for regional integration and cooperation; and (3) borders as barriers and possible causes of conflicts and\or violence.

The focus here is on the first approach, which views borders as activities, processes and discourses. This approach helps us to explore border narratives and ethnogenesis from the perspective of the Nyangatom living in the warscape of Ethiopia–Kenya–South Sudan.

The following article is divided into two major sections, followed by some brief concluding remarks. Part one focuses on providing the historical background that helps explain the forms of interaction that have emerged between the Nyangatom and external groups, including the Ethiopian state. Part two then provides a discussion of anthropological approaches in the study of borders and the shifting trend in analyses toward the activities, discourses and processes involving people residing in and around border areas. In this section, empirical evidence – such as the day-to-day activities of individuals living in and around the Ilemi Triangle[1], their narratives and the stories they tell amongst each other – is provided to show how borders have shaped the experience

1 The Ilemi Triangle is a large segment of land adjoining Ethiopia, Kenya and South Sudan. Until recently, the area served as a grazing land for pastoralists residing on the peripheries of these countries.

of the Nyangatom over time. A brief explanation of the Nyangatom perception of the Ethiopian state and vice versa is also included.

The data for the paper was collected using ethnographic fieldwork methods, including interviews, field observation and review of archival sources.[2] The discussion will also be supported by empirical evidence collected during research in 2011 and 2012.

Aspects of the Relationship Between the Ethiopian State and Local People

Two basic views of Emperor Menelik II's campaign of conquest, which led to the incorporation of the people of the south and southwestern provinces and the creation of the modern Ethiopian state in the late nineteenth century, seem to have emerged. First is the assumption, held by most historians, that the customs and lifestyles of the people of the newly incorporated areas were thought, by the forces of Menelik and the subsequent Ethiopian administrators from the centre, to be inferior and that that people were in need of salvation and that Menelik's campaign of conquest was justified as incorporation (Bahru 1991; Bulatovich 2000). This view portrays Menelik's campaign of conquest in a positive light. Second is the view held mainly by anthropologists, who interpret the conquest as internal colonialism (Sisay and Holcomb 1990; Asmerom 2001). While the first school of thought stresses nation-building and nationalism, the latter concentrates on the experience of local people during and immediately after the conquest.

Both archival sources and oral histories indicate the fact that the pastoralists of the southwestern region experienced a number of ups and downs. There were violent encounters with the forces of Menelik II before the state managed to exert its influence via taxation in the years after the area was incorporated by his successors. Taxation, however, never meant a peaceful relationship between the local people in general, and the Nyangatom in particular, and the Ethiopian state.

Furthermore, archival sources reveal protracted border negotiation between the Ethiopian state and the then colonial administrators of British East Africa and the Sudan. The Ilemi Triangle had become a bone of contention between the two parties, and most official meetings between the British – and, after independence, the Kenyan and Sudanese – authorities indicate a lack of agreement as to the exact location of the border between the three nation states. Official documents from the imperial regime take Ileret, Nabremus and the River Kibish as the limits of the border between Kenya and Ethiopia. But Nyangatom informants claim that their territory extends deep into what is now the Kenyan province of Lokichokiyo Natera.

Most government documents from the imperial period[3] indicate that Kenyan and Ethiopian officials held frequent meetings (especially in the period between 1940 and late 1960s), mainly about cooperation between the two governments in identifying local people who had crossed the border and evaded taxes. In the interviews I carried out for this research, Nyangatom elders denied these allegations and even claimed that they had never evaded the taxes imposed by successive regimes. Instead, they complained about

2 These are written documents (primary sources) from Jinka municipality, the National Museum of Addis Ababa and Wolde Meskel Archive that I collected over the course of researching for a PhD dissertation at the University of Bergen between 2010 and 2016.

3 These are primary sources produced during the imperial period in various government offices.

a lack of state support for their cause in the face of frequent attacks from Kenya and curtailment of their freedom to routinely move across the border.

One archival source[4] indicates that Nyangatom had crossed into Sudanese territory, thus avoiding taxes. In the report produced by the concerned tax collector, the religion of the local chief in question was described as *aremene* (literally 'uncivilized savage'). This source may support the argument of those who portray the campaign of Menelik as internal colonialism, aimed amongst other things at 'bringing the uncivilized into light'. Similarly, one elderly informant related how he collaborated with Ethiopian state representatives and was converted to Orthodox Christianity: the culmination of the civilizing mission of the Ethiopian authorities. Thus, it could be said that the authority of the Ethiopian government – like that of the European powers in the late nineteenth and twentieth century's – was mainly felt through some form of administrative presence, predominantly in the form of taxation, in almost all frontier regions.

Borders as Activities, Processes and Discourses

Until recently, border studies paid little attention to the complex activities and processes that take place along border areas (Baud and van Schendel 1997; Paasi 1998). As Baud and van Schendel have stated:

> There is an extensive literature on how the states have dealt with their borderlands, but historians have paid much less attention to how borderlands have dealt with their states. As a result, borderlands have been represented as far more passive and re-active than is warranted. The study of borderlands assigns an active historical role to borderlands and their population. The purpose is to redress the imbalance of 'state-centred' studies, and to discover which social impulses originated in the borderlands and what effects they had locally as well as beyond the borderland (1997: 235).

In their introduction to *Anthropology in the margins of the state*, Das and Poole (2004) argue for a thorough examination of marginal practices, places and languages in an attempt to bring the state, which has long been sidelined, back into ethnographies. By using Agamben's notion of exception (Agamben 1942), the editors explore the role of margins as an instrument of exclusion and inclusion. Horstmann (2004) highlights the need to include the voice of borderlanders in the study of state margins. Based on research conducted in Southeast Asian borderlands and the activities of the people on the margins of different states, he suggests the need to explore boundary-crossing practices. Following Paasi (1998), Horstmann asserts that:

> Boundaries and their meanings are historically contingent, and they are part of the production and institutionalization of territories. In this sense all boundaries are socially constructed. Attention should be paid to boundary producing practices and to narratives of inclusion and exclusion (2004: 3).

What is more, the activities of people living on state margins challenge the state monopoly of identification and the accepted concepts of nationalism. The practices of frontier

4 This source is retrieved from the National Archive commonly known as *Womezekir* in Addis, Folder 290: File No. 124. It was a letter written to the Ministry of Interior from a Galab and Hamar Bakko District administrator.

communities are in contradiction with the basic assumptions of social anthropology, which is characterized by the fixed boundaries of the nation state.

This limitation could be addressed by shifting the focus of anthropological investigations away from such widely held assumptions (Radu 2012). Radu argues that it is more fruitful to think of borders as 'actants', instead of viewing them as 'enacted' entities. In this, Radu underscores the view that considers the frontier as having active and agentive capacity in relation to the centre. He then suggests:

> Anthropologists will be more beneficial to borders, and vice versa, if they consider the frontier as processes and activities and redirect a closer look at both internal-personal and relational experiences of crossing and dwelling the frontier in their multiplicity and various scales (Radu 2012: 20).

Radu supports his argument by revealing how the border along the Danube River between Rumania and Yugoslavia has been subject to different interpretations since 1989, when a dam was constructed across the border. The dam and the opening of the border coincided with the collapse of socialism, which in turn enhanced the interaction of the borderlanders, who have different interpretations of their own day-to-day encounters.

In spite of the poor infrastructure along the Ilemi Triangle connecting the borderlands of Ethiopia, Kenya and South Sudan, individuals there have been actively engaged in a web of relationships. Most Nyangatom people on the Ethiopian side have relatives living across the borders, either in northwest Kenya or in southeast South Sudan. The patterns of these relationships can be expressed in different forms. It is not uncommon to meet individuals who spend some time in southeast South Sudan among their Nyangatom and Toposa[5] kin. For example, one young Nyangatom informant, interviewed in June 2012, explained how he managed to make a living by moving across and along the border: 'I used to sell local liquor for Toposa militia in exchange for bullets; and upon my return to home, I sold the bullets to Suri[6] pastoralists in Ethiopia.' This is just one example of how some Nyangatom have managed to manipulate their location along the international border and acted as intermediaries between the Toposa and the Suri.

Yet, since 1989[7] the Ilemi Triangle and specifically the River Kibish has become a constraint, which the Nyangatom people may not cross as usual. Their movement and exchange activities have been curtailed by the Kenyan authorities and surrounding Turkana pastoralists. According to Nyangatom borderlanders, the porous border has even become an excuse for sudden Kenyan attacks in the form of cattle raids. Most Nyangatom informants feel that the failure of the Ethiopian state to secure the border has made their situation miserable. While Kenyan troops are always on the other side of the border, acting as a watchdog, until recently there were no security guards to be seen on the Ethiopian side. This has created an environment conducive to cattle raiding by the Turkana and Kenyan soldiers. During field research, I witnessed a number of occasions when

5 The Toposa are one of the groups called *ateker* (commonly known as Karimojong Cluster), and they have a peaceful relationship with the Nyangatom.

6 The Suri are a small agro-pastoral group living north of the Nyangatom.

7 In 1989, just before the final collapse of the *Derg* regime, the Nyangatom were in conflict with their Turkana neighbours. In this conflict, however, the Kenyan government intervened on behalf of Turkana pastoralists and attacked Nyangatom across the border with the help of a helicopter.

Turkana pastoralists launched cattle raids across the River Kibish against the Nyangatom. The absence of state control and support on the Ethiopian side has led most Nyangatom to think that they are neglected by the state, especially in comparison to the support the Turkana receive from the Kenyan government. The cumulative effect of these acts of cattle raiding seems to have been an erosion of the borderlanders' perception of belonging to the Ethiopian state. This, coupled with the relative security and protection that Ethiopian Nyangatom[8] have received from the Sudanese side and their historic ties with the Toposa, has persuaded Nyangatom borderlanders to negotiate their allegiance in favour of the youngest African state, South Sudan. The fact that a large segment of Nyangatom live in South Sudan, makes it easy for those from the Ethiopian side to move to South Sudan. This kind of border crossing might be accompanied by a permanent shift in home base and employment in the Sudanese civil service and bureaucracy.

In addition to the above-mentioned forms of relationship – of trade and conflict – the Ilemi Triangle exhibits a wide variety of interactions among pastoralists inhabiting the area. Here the experience of Merimug is worth mentioning. During my research, he was the only person who adhered to the traditional hair-dressing style for men, using red and white clay for decoration. When asked why he still practiced it, he stated: 'I have still bond friends in Turkana across the border, although Nyangatom no longer cross River Kibish to bring clay, needed for the clay cap, or other commodities inside Turkana territory.' What is perplexing is that, even though he had contacts and bond friends amongst the Turkana, Merimug was killed by these same people in a sudden raid launched by the Turkana early in 2012. Contrasting reactions emerged from Nyangatom informants upon learning of the death of Merimug. One of them – a key informant from the Ngiribo clan, who was a blood relative of the deceased and in charge of the Security Office of Nyangatom *Woreda*[9] – exclaimed, as if he didn't want to believe what happened: '...this is the very first time where I hold grudge against the people of Turkana. How could they kill Merimug in such a way?' Another comment came from an informant from a different territorial section called Ngilignakol and from the Ngidocha clan, who claimed: 'Merimug was killed because he was cursed by Nyangatom people, since they believe that he was collaborating with the Turkana.' He then added:

> Most Nyangatom are happy because he is dead. It was he who was helping Turkana to trace Nyangatom settlements. Imagine he didn't even have a fence for his homestead for he knew that Turkana wouldn't steal his property.

The first case shows how a blood relative of the deceased was hurt by the incident. His opinion also indicates he was ready to forgive the Turkana as long as nobody was killed from his own clan. The latter opinion reveals the other side of the story, suggesting that Merimug's death was a relief since there was a belief among some sections of the society that his action of crossing the border and continuing to foster a relationship with the Turkana was not acceptable at that time. The phrase 'imagine he didn't even have a fence

8 During the Sudanese civil war, Nyangatom communities used to get material support like guns, bullets and the like mainly from the SPLA/M rebels. In some cases, Nyangatom youth were recruited by rebels in the fight against Khartoum.

9 Administrative unit next to *kebele*; *kebele* is the smallest administrative unit in Ethiopia.

for his homestead for he knew that Turkana wouldn't steal his property' indicates that the importance of fences for protecting cattle was well known. Yet, Merimug had none, which contradicted what other sections of the society were doing. His actions were, thus, interpreted differently: he was characterized as a defector, whose death was welcome.

On the surface, Merimug's case shows the extent to which the relationship between Nyangatom and Turkana has become tense around the border. The international border has become a barrier to communication. But, the two different interpretations of Merimug's death also indicate how individuals' perceptions of similar events constitute different border narratives.

Dereje and Hoehne (2008) pinpoint the need to take a look at the opportunities and affordances that borders offer, and at the ways in which the people of borderlands exploit them. According to them, most studies of African borderlands have emphasised the constraints of borders as opposed to the opportunities and the strategies often employed by the inhabitants to make use of them. They give a number of examples of how people along the borders of the Horn of Africa manage to use borders to their own advantage. One example is provided by the Gadabuursi, a Somali clan living along the Ethiopia–Somalia border in the eastern part of Ethiopia. By virtue of their very location along the crossroad of the two countries, the Gadabuursi manage to make economic and political gains from both the Ethiopian government and the British Protectorate of Somaliland in the face of taxation from the two competing powers. For example, effectively exploiting the situation in which they were caught, some members of one Gadabuursi family held an important traditional leadership role in the British Protectorate, while others rose to the position of *dejazmach* (Commander of the Gate) on the Ethiopian side.

Following Feyisa and Hoehne (2008), I contend that the international Ethiopia–Kenya–South Sudan border, along which the Nyangatom are located, offers a number of opportunities for the local people. Of the many affordances the border offers, I want to underscore the political and cultural dimensions in the following.[10] In particular, the birth of South Sudan appears to have been the most important political factor providing new opportunities. Educated Nyangatom from southwest Ethiopia were immediate beneficiaries of South Sudan's emergence, as some of them got the opportunity to join high-up government offices in South Sudan's bureaucracy. The case of the State Minister of Environment, Wildlife Conservation and Tourism in South Sudan (in 2012) illustrates this. He is a Nyangatom by birth, attended Sudanese elementary schools, was educated at university in Kenya, and served as a civil servant during the *Derg* regime in Ethiopia (1974–91). He then fled Ethiopia in 1995, and joined the Sudan People's Liberation Army (SPLA) during the height of the civil war in the Sudan. He, along with many other Nyangatom youth, either spent their formative years in SPLA-controlled South Sudan or directly participated in the war, standing side-by-side with the southern rebels. Similarly, some Nyangatom civil servants working in Nyangatom *Woreda* received their education in South Sudan or Kenya, in places such as Narus and Kapoeta. It seems clear that cross-border mobility offers multiple choices and opportunities not only with regard to employment, but also education.

10 Economic status and rights resources seem to have been outweighed by the political and cultural opportunities. For more, see the introduction section by Dereje and Hoehne (2008).

Returning to Dereje and Hoehne (2008: 11), we find a situation where the Anywaa and the Nuer ethnic groups inhabiting the western Ethiopia–Sudan border are using citizenship as a means of inclusion and exclusion. When the Ethiopian Empire and the British agreed the boundary in 1902, the majority of the Anywaa resided in Ethiopia, with some groups living in the Sudan, while most of the Nuer became residents of the Sudan and only a small section remained in Ethiopia. However, since the EPRDF came to power in Ethiopia in1991 and adopted a policy of ethnic federalism, the Anywaa have begun to question whether the Nuer qualify for Ethiopian citizenship; and some have gone further, considering the Nuer to be 'foreigners'. Today the major political debate in the state of Gambela in Ethiopia is about who is a citizen or who is not.

In the discussion above, we have seen a few ethnographic cases that might reflect the ways in which the Ilemi Triangle (as an international border) shapes the different activities and narratives of the Nyangatom. However, focusing on the lives of Nyangatom and their relationship with other groups living nearby may not allow us to see the bigger picture: the role and perception of the state toward local people and vice versa.

In this regard, it is crucial to revisit what Donham (2002) once underscored in his introduction to *Southern marches of imperial Ethiopia: Essays in history and social anthropology*. According to Donham, seen from the perspective of the salient developments of late nineteenth-century Ethiopia, the notion of 'frontier' seems to be a relevant analytical concept. The modern Ethiopian state is a product of a series of campaigns of conquest launched by the forces of Menelik II (1889–1906). The newly conquered places of the southern and southwestern provinces were called Dar Ager. Dar Ager is an Amharic term that can be literally translated as 'fringe territory' or 'frontier province' (Donham 2002; Tsega-Ab 2005).

Since then, historians have examined the peoples of the southern and southwestern provinces from the perspective of the centre; whereas anthropologists have been inclined to consider peoples of peripheral areas as distinct categories. Nevertheless, for Donham (2002) the situation represents a confrontation of power between the centre and the periphery. Accordingly, using 'frontier' as an analytical concept enables us to bring the history and anthropology of Ethiopia together. The notion of 'frontier', with its emphasis on cultural contact, helps to bridge the gap between the existing historical and anthropological studies. Yet, Donham's analytical reflection does not provide an adequate explanation of the confusing and often misleading concepts of 'frontier'. Instead, 'frontier' was suggested as a remedy for the existing problem of centre–periphery relations in the context of Ethiopia in general. Still, it seems apparent that Donham implicitly acknowledges the salient feature of 'frontier', as the term was originally used by Frederick J. Turner in 1893, that is as a centrifugal and 'outer edge of a wave – the meeting point between savagery and civilization' (Rankin and Schofield 2004: 4).

In other words, this indicates that starting from the time of incorporation there seems to have been two slightly different ways of treating the peoples of the southern and southwestern periphery. Historians are inclined towards the study of the newly incorporated people from the perspective of the centre, whereas anthropologists are more interested in dealing with the peoples and cultures of the inhabitants of the southern and southwestern areas in isolation.

Concluding Remarks

The foregoing has discussed the complex ways in which borders, in particular the Ilemi Triangle, shape the experiences of the Nyangatom living along the crossroads of Ethiopia–Kenya–South Sudan. By adopting an approach which views borders as activities, processes and discourses, I have explored how the Ilemi Triangle became an axis for various forms of relationship among inhabitants of the region. In some cases, the Ilemi Triangle has become a source for cooperation, as Nyangatom traverse the international border to visit kin residing on the other side and even establish close ties when individuals decide to migrate. In other circumstances, the Ilemi Triangle has become the source of constrained relationships between Nyangatom and their surrounding neighbours, when conflicts break out among groups.

The conflicting and contradicting narratives embedded in the long history of the relationship between the Ethiopian state and the Nyangatom of the Lower Omo Valley have also been explored. The history of Ethiopian state formation and the power struggle of the late nineteenth century among various groups in the region have played an important role in shaping the perception of Nyangatom toward the state and vice versa.

References

AGAMBEN Giorgio

1942 (1998) *Homo sacer. Sovereign power and bare life.* Stanford: Stanford University Press.

ASMEROM Legesse

2001 *Oromo democracy: An indigenous African political system.* Lawrenceville: The Red-Sea Press.

BAHRU Zewde

1991 *A history of modern Ethiopia 1855–1974.* Addis Ababa: Addis Ababa University Press.

BAUD, Michiel and Willem VAN SCHENDEL

1997 'Toward a comparative history of borderlands', *Journal of World History* 8(2): 211–242.

BROCH-DUE, Vigdis

1990 *The bodies within the body: Journeys in Turkana thought and practice.* PhD Dissertation, University of Bergen.

BULATOVICH, Aleksander

2000 *Ethiopia through Russian eyes: Country in transition 1896–1898.* Lawrenceville, Asmara: The Red Sea Press.

DAS, Veena and Deborah POOLE

2004 *Anthropology in the margins of the State.* Santa Fe: School of American Research Press.

DEREJE Feyissa and Markus HOEHNE

2008 'Resourcing state borders and boundaries in the Horn of Africa', *Max Planck Institute for Social Anthropology Working paper 107.*

DONHAM, Donald

2002 'The making of an imperial state: Old Abyssinia and the new Ethiopian empire. Themes in social history', in: Donald L. Donham and Wendy James (eds.), *Southern marches of imperial Ethiopia: Essays in history and social anthropology*, 3–50. Oxford: James Curry.

ELIAS Alemu

2016 *Living on the margin: Masculinity, violence and development intervention among Nyangatom, Southwestern Ethiopia.* PhD thesis, University of Bergen.

HOLCOMB, Bonnie K. and SISAY Ibsa

1990 *The invention of Ethiopia.* Lawrenceville: The Red Sea Press.

HORSTMANN, Alexander

2004 *Incorporation and resistance, transnational communities and social change in Southeast Asia.* Oxford: ERSC Communities Programme, Working Paper WPTC-02-04.

PAASI, Anssi

1998 'Boundaries as social processes: Territoriality in the world of flows', *Geopolitics* 3(1): 69–88.

RADU, Cosmin

2012 'Frontier effects and tidemarks: A commentary in the anthropology of borders', in: Massimo Canevacci (ed.), *Polyphonic anthropology: Theoretical and empirical cross-cultural fieldwork*, 19–32. London: IntechOpen.

RANKIN, K.J. and Richard N. SCHOFIELD

2004 'The troubled historiography of classical boundary terminology', *IBIS Working Papers 41.*

TESHOME Wondwosen

2009 'Colonial boundaries of Africa: The case of Ethiopia's boundary with Sudan', *Ege Akademik Bakis* 9(1): 337–367.

TSEGA-AB, Kassa

2005 *An administrative history of Galab and Hamar-Bakko Awraja southwestern Ethiopia: Political and cultural contact 1941–1974.* MA thesis, Addis Ababa University.

TURNER, Frederick Jackson

1893 *The Significance of the frontier in American history.* Madison: State Historical Society of Wisconsin.

Folk Media as a Platform for Conflict Resolution

The Case of Gedeo, Ethiopia

NIGUSSIE MESHESHA

Background

The study of conflict resolution has become a major concern for academics and research institutions due to its political and social significance for many peoples. Consequently, researchers from various disciplines – including communication and media studies – have studied conflict resolution from different perspectives. It is believed that, although conflicts arise for different reasons, a key feature is the breakdown in communication between the parties involved. This is because communication is the lubricant, or fuel, for any social process, but its poor handling can create social friction and lead to conflict.

Consequently, studying the communication system of a people in lieu of conflict resolution becomes highly important because, first, it is thought that the people's communication system provides the better way to address conflicts that occur in a society. Second, the people do value their cultural communication system in resolving conflicts more than what has been induced by the modern legal system. Second, the people mostly use their customary practices so as to come up with pragmatic solutions for the conflicts that break out. Third, the people's communication system is central to them so as to resolve conflicts in a socially acceptable and natural setting of the people. Finally, the overall rubric of the political, social and cultural system is tied up to the folk ways of the people, which are revealed through their communication system. From this vantage point, it is appropriate to see the folk communication system in general and their folk media in particular as part of their customary practices.

Mainly, the study of folk media is useful since it is a forum of public discussion and debate like what is done by the modern media. Folk media provides the platform for social interaction and the means through which cohesion is maintained, consensus created, and cultural values reinforced (Tadesse 2004; Finnegan 2012). This media can be used in the society in the act of bridging the leeway in the overall political, social and cultural process. Though there are disagreements about what folk media are, they can be best understood as indigenous equivalents of exogenous mass media (Valbuena 1986; Nigussie and Yri 2016). They include the rituals, festivals, plays, puppet shows, dance, song, storytelling, poetry and others used in different social practices (Finnegan 2012). These folk media are 'the corpus of orally transmitted [communicated] material which address [...] specifically to the recounting of the past' (Vansina 1985: 13), but much relevance to the current life.

The place of folk media in conflict resolution can be better understood from our understanding of what causes conflicts. Basically, the causes of conflict are varied, but communication gap takes the major part. Some conflicts are linked to human nature, that is, to people's physical and psychological needs and the gap between expectations and materializations. Some are caused by economic, value and power factors (Fisher 2000). Competition for resources certainly plays a part, but value and power conflict are often intertwined and sometimes predominate. Economic conflict involves competing motives to attain scarce resources. Value conflict involves incompatibility in ways of life, ideologies – the preferences, principles and practices that people believe in, and power conflict occurs when each party wishes to maintain or maximize the amount of influence that it exerts in a particular relationship and social setting, which can be resolved through effective communication.

At the same time, Fisher has identified conflicts occurring at the interpersonal, intergroup, multiparty and international levels, which bring communication as a central point (Fisher 2000). Interpersonal conflict occurs when two people have incompatible needs, goals, or approaches; it is marked by a communication breakdown. Role conflict involves very real differences in role definitions, expectations or responsibilities between individuals who are interdependent in a social system. Intergroup conflict occurs between collections of people, such as ethnic or racial groups, between departments or levels of decision-making in the same organization, and between unions and management. Multi-party conflict occurs when different interest groups and organizations in a society have varying priorities over resource management and policy development. International conflict occurs between states at the global level (Fisher 2000). In all cases, negotiation is one of the major characteristics of customary or traditional approaches to conflict resolution. The study presented here suggests that alternative methods often produce more satisfactory results and are more efficient than modern or legal methods in negotiating settlements to disputes, even though there it could be contended that 'alternative dispute resolution techniques may lead as readily to socially unjust outcomes' (Shmueli u.d).

This indicates that cultural, social and political problems are resolved using traditional cultural and communication means. As a result of this, the present study emphasizes the use of folk media for maintaining peace and order among the Gedeo people. This is done by investigating how folk media is used as the platform for addressing political, social and cultural matters. There are, of course, situations in which the folk media is used differently, for example, to perpetuate stereotypes and prejudices (Finnegan 2012), but such acts are little appreciated in societies as it is evident in the 'modern' media. Generally, however, folk media are useful for maintaining social cohesion and helping to avoid conflicts since they are often used in the various conflict resolution or settlement mechanisms.

Problem statement

The Gedeo people are known to have long-standing cultural and social practices that are transmitted through the generations through their folk ways, which are woven into their way of life. This is evident in their cultural and ritualistic activities, agro-ecological practices, and historical heritages, whose cultural, social and political significance is expressed in their folk media.

There are a handful of studies on the indigenous agro-ecological practices and cultural and historical heritages of the Gedeo. Most of these focus on the people's knowledge system and agro-ecological practices. Yirefu, Wondawek and Bogale (2016), for instance, have studied the woody plant species grown in the different agro-forestry zones managed by the Gedeo, thereby indicating the indigenous agro-ecological practices of the people. Setegn et. al. (2016) have studied the reaction of Gedeo farmers to newly introduced water and soil conservation practices, eventually suggesting that there was a need to adapt these new practices to the local practices of the people. Getachew and Mamo (2015) have studied the Gedeo's indigenous ecological knowledge system and local ecological management. Birhane and Melesse (2015) have made an evaluative study of the Gedeo's land-use patterns in different agro-ecological and slope classes. Meanwhile, Kiros, Samuel and Dagne (2014) have researched the Gedeo community's living situations and highlighted the cultural, biological and socio-economic perspectives of the people. Abiyot, Bogale and Baudouin (2013) have undertaken a study on the indigenous agroforestry knowledge transfer system, focusing on the youth in Wonago Woreda, Gedeo Zone. Finally, Mesele (2007) has studied the management and livelihoods of Gedeo's agro-forests, focusing on the ecological knowledge system and indigenous practices.

With regard to the topic under consideration here, Wedekind (1977) can be mentioned for his analysis of Gedeo work songs in the context of the 1974 Ethiopian revolution. As can Asebe's (2007) analysis of the ethnicity and inter-ethnic relations between the Guji and Gedeo. Even so, aside from some attempts made by undergraduate students in various universities in Ethiopia, only a limited amount of research can be found on socio-cultural and literary aspects of the Gedeo. In particular, there has been no study to date on the folk media and communication practices of the people. This is the gap that this study aims to fill.

Objectives

The general objective of this study is to analyse the use of folk media as the platform for the Gedeo's conflict resolution practices. Specifically, the study aims to:

- reveal how the Gedeo use their folk media as a platform for conflict resolution;
- indicate the role of folk media in social mobilization and change among the people;
- identify whether the people prefer the use of folk media over modern approaches to conflict resolution.

Theoretical and conceptual framework

This study is grounded in narrative theory and the theory of discourse analysis. According to narrative theory, people tell stories to do some kind of actions. Johnstone (2004) highlights cross-cultural differences in the functions of narrative, drawing on the work of Scollon and Scollon (1981), who claim that stories are the primary source of knowledge as reality is socially constructed through narrative. Folk narratives carry the same or similar meaningful actions, helping the Gedeo convey social messages like that of the modern media, making narrative theory particularly relevant. As is discourse theory, whose 'basic premise', according to Karlberg (2005: 1), is 'the ways we think and talk about a subject influence and reflect the ways we act in relation to that subject'. The discourse made in orally transmitted messages is contained in the speech we utter, and tells the conventionality, actuality and intentionality of the speech. This is based on John Austin's idea of the speech situation as outlined in his speech act theory; according to which, there must exist an accepted conventional procedure having a certain conventional effect where certain words are uttered by certain persons in certain circumstances, and further, some action is invoked with certain thoughts and feelings to convey some meanings in the participants' minds (Oishi 2006).

Materials and methods

The study took place in Dilla and Wenago towns for a period of four weeks and was undertaken with the financial support of Hawassa University. The methodology of the study includes data collection through interviews, focus group discussion in the field and participant observation in social settings, such as during various folk performances. Local elders, traditional religious leaders, and experts from cultural bureau were interviewed. Elders and cultural club members from Gedeo Zone were included in focus group discussions. The snowball sampling method was used to find people who were knowledgeable in describing or performing cultural practices. Finally, important socio-cultural songs and performances were recorded, transcribed and translated with the help of a translator who has linguistic and cultural competence. The data were then interpreted and thematically analysed.

Analysis and Discussion

Folk media and history

Folk media is the platform by which the Gedeo people tell their history. According to their oral folk stories, the Gedeo people came from a place called Harsunke, south of their current land, and settled in the area of Hawaxxa around Ballayyaa – which is around Bulle Woreda. The oral history of the people offers no indication of the time when the Gedeo people came from Harsunke and settled at Hawaxxa.[1]

According to their folk communications, the Gedeo people settled in their current place in perhaps the sixteenth century, and perhaps in connection with the movement of the Sidaama and the Oromo. In other words, their settlement situation today could possibly be related to the movement of the Oromo and the settlement of the Sidaama in the highlands east of Abaya Lake and west of the Bale Oromo. The Gedeo origin myth is communicated to the young through the following folksong:

Harrsunki fuleeni Hawaxxa dangenni.	From Harsunke [they] came to Hawatta.
No'o jelaatee kea	With feast they moved to.
Ho! Ho! Ho!	Ho! Ho! Ho!

Today, the Gedeo live in the Southern Nations Nationalities People Regional State (SNNPRS) in the vicinity of Dilla, which is the capital of Gedeo Zone as it is currently constituted by the Federal Democratic Republic of Ethiopia (EPRDF). They were formerly under Sidamo province, which was called Gedeo Awraja. Their language is Gedeogna. Though some say the Gedeo's ancestry is not well known, others trace their origin to the aboriginal tribe called Murgga-Gosallo (Tadesse 2002: 22), perhaps the earliest people to have lived in the area. The Gedeo elders also tell that Gedeo have descended

1 An old Gedeo man, about 70 years old, and others in closer age groups narrated the history of the Gedeo in a marketplace in Wenago.

from the ancestral roots through their social grading. The people installed their own *baalle* (social grading), a tradition similar to the *gada* tradition of the Oromo, which is a system of government based on grades and ranks according to age classes (Tadesse 2002).

Gedeo society, folk media and conflict resolution

Gedeo folk stories do indicate the interrelationships among the clans in the society. The Gedeo tell that they have seven clans, which are classified into two groups: *sholle baaxxee* (group of four) and *sassee baaxxee* (group of[1]three).[2] The clans are Darasha, Gorgorsha, Daba'a, Hanuma, which form the group of four, and Lomeda, Henba and Bakarro, the group of three. According to respondents from all the subgroups, Darasha is the most respected and privileged subgroup among the Gedeo. In Gedeo's mythology, the Darasha is ranked highest in Gedeo's clan hierarchy. Respect for the subgroups depends on their position in this hierarchy. After Darasha comes Gorgorsha, Daba'a and so on until Bakaro, which has the least respect. Tadesse (2002: 23) mentions these hierarchical relations and social relations, stating that Daraso, the founding father, is said to have had seven sons from two wives. From these were descended the seven Gedeo tribes: Daba'a, Darasha, Gorgorsha, Hanuma, Bakaro, Henbba'a and Logoda. These are organized into two classes or 'houses': *sholle baaxxee* (the senior), to which the first four belong, and *sassee baaxxee* (the junior), to which the last three belong.

Though there is no concrete evidence for this division into two groups, some mythological sources indicate that the formation of these hierarchies was probably the cause of conflict between the *sholle baaxxee* and the *sassee baaxxee* over boundaries and ownership of resources.

Conflicts in Gedeo can be grouped into different types: domestic, boundary, etc. The traditional conflict resolution of the Gedeo is performed at *roga* (district administrator) level. The cases are brought to *ardenxxe* (local elders), who cross check the ill deeds and sinful acts.

The *hutetiki hyiticha* (chief judicial administrator) of the *roga* acts as chief judicial functionary within the *gosa* (group) and works in collaboration with lower *hyiticha* (wise men or leaders) on appeals drawn from sub-clans. Being close to the society, the assistant *hyiticha* services play a role in the societies about their spiritual and social wellbeing. They examine the nature of any conflict and try to settle low-level quarrels and disagreements in their administrative domains at the *songo* (gathering). This is, of course, communicated to the society at large using the existing hierarchy.

Each of the *songo* has its own successors, called *batitiki hyiticha* (village level administrator), and its *dobalicha* (prospective successor) and *mura* (local messengers). The *batitiki hyiticha* works under the *huletiki hyiticha* (land administrator /allocates land). The local elders usually assist the *batitiki hyiticha*, who judges in cases of martial conflict, boundary quarrels, destruction of wealth, theft or assault.

The conflicts among the Gedeo people are usually resolved within the administrative circle. The Gedeo *gada* system also works in the domain of the *hyiticha* who are chosen

2 *Sholle baaxxee* and *sassee baaxxee* indicate the social organization and the communication system of the Gedeo.

based on the number of the clans. If the number of the clans is many, the number of *hyiticha* will increase with their social organization. This can be related to the modern representative form of government. Then, the folk media are used for conflict resolution within the involvement of the *roga*, the *hyiticha* and *ardenxxee*. This is done by folk media such as folk narration at the social and political gathering, the *songo*.

The Gedeo's approach to conflict resolution is often culturally valued by the people, and according to the research informants it is found to be highly useful in settling disputes over marriage relationships, farm boundaries and boundary disputes among the sub clans, clans and ethnic groups. This indicates that the Gedeo prefer to use their strong social institutions to resolve conflicts using institutional rules and norms. These institutional rules and norms are established and maintained through the orally communicated messages using indigenous communication platforms, which can be labeled as folk media. The people have their own well-established traditions of governance and communication systems, which generally enable them to accommodate peacefully to change, unlike those who do not have this and are more likely to buckle. This demonstrates that the folk media has a central place in Gedeo because they use their folk media for resolving various types of disputes in the society.

Resolving marriage conflicts

Conflicts within married couples are resolved at many levels. For example, the husband may try to suppress a misunderstanding with his wife by persuading her, by punishing her or by advising her with the help of his family. However, if the conflict cannot be resolved at home, it will be taken to the local elders. Mostly it is the woman who presents her case to the local elders and, after listening to her case, the elders interrogate the husband over his maltreatment of his wife. The wife might say he severely hit her, insulted her, etc. Based on the words of the wife, the elders ask him if he has committed the crime or not. In fact, the husband never denies the crime because to do so would bring misfortune in his life, wealth, or children. Hence, he confesses, but he defends him by claiming that he did it because she does not serve him food properly or on time, she comes home late, she lies to him, and so on. Depending on the graveness of the matter, the elders advise and order both of them to be good husband and wife. Then, the husband is required to ask for an apology and then the elderly give their blessings for a happy life, to bear children, etc.

However, if the wife is dissatisfied with her husband because he has married another wife, the elders ask the husband why he did so. The husband says that he married again because his first wife does not serve him food, is preoccupied with house chores and childcare, is infertile, etc. Having examined the case and learned the truth of the husband's claims, a decision is made to resolve the conflict. In most cases, the husband is not punished,[3] but if the elders find out his failure to meet his wife's wants after discussions with her family and his, he will be made to pay *murra* (compensation). Usually the women do not take every issue to the verdict of the local jury or the elderly; they rather express their dissatisfaction through insulting and sometimes cursing of their husbands using oral songs, as a psychological communication or approach to console themselves through a kind of intrapersonal communication.

3 Polygyny is allowed to the husband, if the woman fails to meet her husband's needs.

The following folksong epitomizes the psychological communication approach to dispute resolution. This song is often sung by youth and women when they perform housework, do agricultural activities, or sit together. Through the song, they criticize those who go to urban areas and do something considered as a social taboo. Those who do so are often considered to have demeaned the culture and such acts often lead to ostracization. This is actually to teach the women to act positively in her marriage and even the man is allowed to punish her if she shows ill acts.

Dilli manna	People of Dilla
Dillassine meluu ganna	They hit their women /hit them "dill!"
C'affee beele	is there
Melalle birte uteele	The women finish up the hotel's food
Koo Gonnocco	You, Gonnocco,
Gobake'ni gannassi odolco	put the pot round your neck!
Haweyyo hawee	You have you
Hawawi sa'ne gadoogali	You spent the night shouting outside people of Dilla, you can't hit the women who is out of her mind

In the above folk poem, it is possible to say that the husband can punish his wife if he finds her doing wrong. As a conflict resolution system, such media are used to convince either party to be obedient to the culture. Those women who eat in hotels are cursed for their actions as is customary and may be banishment from their village or community. Women, on the other hand, express their dissatisfaction and explain why they may be quarrelsome using a different folksong:

Daamme da'enneki bulle afebaa.	The stone I grind on has no flour.
Heerunmenne manji butte afebaa.	The man I married has no property.
Badala da'enne gummatika.	I grind maize for your feast.
Badadee afenne summa atika.	I got your name in trouble.
Baabbicco marraatti' dikko hiyyote.	B.- to go there means to go to the market.
anti'i dayyo dagge, Lippo-yyote.	My sister L. came.
Gomara hinjaaladdu qee'lo malee'e.	I don't like those who marry except for the youngest (He's big but bad).
Aayya baddu.	I am sorry (in Guji-Oromo).

The discourse in this folk media is about a woman's dissatisfaction at home as a result of poverty and her husband's incapacity to feed his family. The women in Gedeo use folk media for socializing the young and as informational and mobilization tools. Usually media has informational, educational, correlation or socializing, continuity of cultures, entertainment and social mobilization functions (McQuail 2000). The women vent their grievances using the poem. In reality, the social and cultural injustice felt by the women, as depicted in the poem, is not heard. Consequently, through the poem, the women oppose this cultural silence by questioning the culture and refusing to accept its continuity. Thus, the poem is used to call for social change and challenge the status quo. Similar cultural practices can be seen among adjacent ethnic groups like the Guji Oromo (Tadesse 2004).[4]

The Gedeo women also use poetry to show their role as equal contributors to society.

Labbalinssha hunji inda	Like men we work and eat
Labbalinssha	You men
Faraccokee ora qolce	The horse runs along the way
Koo Halacayyee Abba Doggee	You H. father of D.
Aloo Shaafee	It is very nice
Gogee Golloo	(Name)
Hallo Shaafee Faraccikee	Your horse is brave
Oo! hayyaa	Oh! Sorry

The poem was recorded in the marketplace in Wonago town. The song is usually sung by women to criticize social inequality. The poem indicates the psychological conflict that women face as the dominated. The discourse is about the braveness of men and implies that women have the capacity to behave like men. Even though it is played from men's perspective, the poem demonstrates women's perception about their inequality to men. The superior and subordinate relations seem to have led to psychological conflict between them, and the conflict is only resolved through conforming to the existing power structure.

Marriage in Gedeo is a blessing and there is particularly great respect for fertile women. As the women are said to give birth to *gada* (a king), they have respect from their clan or society, but it seems true that their voices are not heard. The above poems indicate that songs are the means through which women condemn, insult and sometimes curse men for the ill treatment of women. One can take folk songs or poems as weapons of the weak, as a medium for addressing their problems. There are conditions under which a woman may get some kind of compensation – such as new clothes from her husband – through the Gedeo' conflict resolution process. The elders often belief that she became quarrelsome because of her husband's failure to comply with the family's needs. This suggests that males' economic domination often leads to women's subordination, and to conflict. The conflict is resolved sometimes through negotiation between the parties, and often with the mediation of the local elders. In the process, different folk media – such as oral stories and poems – are used to educate, inform and sometimes warn the offender so that the victim's physical and psychological wound is healed. Such folk media are also used to convince the wife. This is the common form of resolving family conflicts in Gedeo because the women prefer abide by the customary practices to resort to modern legal practices. In the cases of serious family conflicts that involve relatives or neighbours, *malawo* (a local drink made of honey) is served to the parties and

4 This connection is epitomized by a distinct linguistic feature observed in the poem: the use of *aayya baddu*, which has a close phonemic link to *aayyabade* (meaning 'I am sorry') in Oromo language. Though this is just one instance, it would, perhaps, be possible to determine through a study of etymology of words and linguistic structure that there is relationship between the Gedeo and the Oromo languages. In a similar vein, Wedekind (1977: 7) states that: 'The closest relations of the Gedeo people have always been those to the Guji people. Gedeo songs have to a large extent been borrowed from the Guji inventory, and the texts of many Gedeo songs contain Guji words.'

the elders after the issue is resolved. The *malawo* is usually a symbolic communication about the peace achieved and the sweetness of life afterwards.

Resolving Boundary Conflict

The system for resolving boundary conflicts is different. Usually the people of the neighbourhood are called to the *songo*.[5] According to Tadesse (2000: 27), 'Gedeo always refer to the *mageno* (the creator) who created these beings (rivers, hills or trees)' and the *songo* in each Gedeo village calls for *mageno* whenever conflicts arise in their locality. This is done by mass *qeexala* (prayer), directed towards resolving conflicts. On such occasions, the elders and *hyiticha* (people of wit) are invited. As a conflict resolving mechanism the case is brought in front of *rago* (the leader or the successor) and the elderly fathers. The *huletiki hyiticha* and *batitiki hyiticha* sit in the adjudication place at the centre, with the opponents sitting on either side. The accuser presents his words and case and, based on his words, the accused defends or accepts the claim. The elders consult the *hyiticha* and determine the guilt or otherwise of the accused.

Depending on the nature of the conflict and its seriousness, the elders decide to demand *murra* (compensation) or draw up the correct boundaries. If one of the parties does not accept the decision reached by the elders, he is excommunicated from the clan. So everybody abides by the *serra* – the social laws or regulations of the group.

The *hultetiki hyiticha* are responsible for allocating land and for deciding on any kind of conflicts over land within the society. However, in fact, farm boundary conflicts between two are more or less resolved by local elders. The local elders lay down stones to mark the boundary mark, cursing anyone who throws the stones away, saying:

Kinjjioo gosshittikee gooshommi	The one who throws away the stones
Lemissetekee leemiattii	Be cursed and thrown out of life

As the society fears the curses of elderly people, nobody dares to defy them. After the elders make the demarcation, they give their blessings, which everyone accepts. If someone does disobey the decisions reached, the fear that something bad will occur is strengthened by the proverb:

Galddee galdamalle	It could be late
Haree warrabe sinittee	But it occurs one day donkey is the dinner for hyena

The proverb is told as a warning that disobedience will lead to some kind of disaster sooner or later.

Boundary conflicts between two individuals can be a source of conflict between clans. The mechanism for resolving clan conflicts will be discussed in the following section.

Resolving Clan Conflict

Clan relations and community affairs do have deeper meanings to the Gedeo. According to Wedekind (1977: 32):

5 It literally denotes meeting, but can be taken as a participatory communication media used to resolve social conflicts and other issues.

> ... the Gedeo texts – more than texts from other cultures – are concerned with "Community" (other persons, social places), with the "Social negative" (anger, sadness, attack, destruction, death and difficulties, and negative evaluation in general).

Wedekind states that the Gedo texts focus on 'getting and retaining' and 'family' (kin, children). Thus, this reveals that clan relations have an important place in the society. According to informants, as it was discussed earlier, the Daraso have seven sons from two wives, who formed the seven Gedeo clans. These are organized into two classes or 'houses': *sholle baaxxee* (the senior), to which the first four belong, and *saasse baaxxee* (the junior), to which the last three belong (Tadesse 2002). The *sholle baaxxee* comprises more than twenty-five sub-classes, and the *saasse baaxxee* consists of ten sub-tribes. In Gedeo, marriage within the same sub-tribe is forbidden. Each of these clans is led by local elders with *hyiticha* and *roga*. The people's social relations and harmony are governed by *serra* (the law). If conflicts exist, the *roga* (the nominated elder) and *hyiticha* sit to decide a solution. The *roga* is the main person in the resolution of disagreements in the *gada* system. The *gada* leads the people and is from a pure family. The person who becomes *gada* is told by *hyiticha* and chosen from the clans. The *gada* can be young, as his appointment is based on lineage and genealogy, and he is the most respected person in the social structure. Nobody, for example, dares to cross the road before the *gada* father. Some sources indicate that once some girls laughed when the *gada* was around them. Then the *gada* cursed the girls, saying:

Laballo hanno hassimalle	Look after men
Laballi hanno hassokkee	Let not men search for you
Tolaango heirumme	Just get married without dowry.

This folk narrative tells about marriage practices among the Gedeo. The discourse is that men took dominion over women. The expression 'look after men' communicates the subordination of female to male in marriage, particularly around the choice of bride and the payment of the dowry, which of course has not exceeded eighty *birr* (local currency) since it was set by the *gada* father. The *gada* curses if someone does wrong, but he blesses positive practices or acts by individuals or groups.

Clan conflicts occur in many ways. One cause could be *bootta* (abduction), which is a form of marriage among the Gedeo. Marriages in Gedeo are not made between members of the same clan; a man must marry a woman from another clan. If a marriage is performed by the will of the female's family where male's family does not come into agreement, it threatens the relationship between the clans and conflict may break out. Those who are from the male's family side destroy houses, cut their rivals' *washo* (enset), take their cattle and herds, etc. When such a conflict occurs, the women in the clans come between the rivals to plead for a peace settlement. Of course, when the women intervene the fighting stops and the parties involved sit for the negotiation with the representatives of the elderly from both clans and the *roga*. Meanwhile, the *gada* father prays to *magano* in thanks for stopping the war. This folk media solution is preferred to the modern legal system.

Resolving Ethnic Conflict

Though the Gedeo share similarities with the Guji, Borana, Arsi and the Sidaama, especially in the structure and function of the *gada* system, they have been involved in a series of conflicts with their neighbouring groups (Asmarom 1973; Tadesse 2004; Lubo 2012). Most of the available narratives and discourses indicate that the Gedeo people have strong links with the Guji and the Sidaama. Tadesse (2002: 25) has noted that 'the Gedeo have maintained close cultural and economic ties with their neighbours, the Guji and the Sidamo'. This is perhaps because the Gedeo are bordered by the Sidaama in the north and the east and by the Guji Oromo in the south and west. However, since the three groups share common boundaries, conflicts occur, mainly over access to grazing land.

As the population of the Gedeo is rapidly increasing because of high fertility, the land in Gedeo is densely populated and each farmer family has only a few hectares of land. At the same time, the adjacent population of the Sidaama fall in shortage of grazing land, and the same goes for the Guji Oromo. This population pressure has resulted in conflict between the neighbouring ethnic groups.

Conflicts can reveal themselves in several ways among these people, but how they are resolved is quite pivotal. The Gedeo have their own conflict resolution mechanisms, based on the culturally constituted institution of the *gada* system as it has been passed through generations using the folktales, folksongs, poems and other folk media. These folkways, among other things, reveal the recurrent conflicts between the Gedeo and the Guji Oromo. For example:

Daddessi dagale	You pound enset
Liqinsi Labane	Drink straight gun
Nunti wore Shaara	We are Shaara people (Nunti-Guji)
Ha'no wofe aada	You should be finished (killed)
Kallacci Gangallo	K. (name)
Maa-ttatte qalqallo?	What do you say, you 'sack' (fat man)?

In the poem, the Gedeo insult and curse their Guji enemies. The poem indicates that the Guji take their land, as enset is an indigenous plant well-known to be a staple food in Gedeo. Enset is preferred by the Gedeo because of the shortage of land (Tadesse 2002: 20). Thus, pounding enset is a very serious matter for the Gedeo. The poem depicts the Guji robbing the Gedeo and taking their property, and reveals the Gedeo desire that they be killed by gun – the gun may symbolize 'war' among the people.

In fact, the Gedeo often express their hatred of their enemies using folk poetry. The following poem reveals this social reality:

Ittettekaa hiissi!	Return what you eat!
Koo Ayyala Siissi!	You destroy Ayele!
Aqurqazhe Siisi!	Destroy the suppressors!
Gattemmatt'a ffiis hoo siis!	Finish the remaining ones!

The discourse in the above is about feudal and tenant relations. *Aqurqazhe* is a borrowed word from Amharic language and is an ideological term, signifying the 'feudal lords' who used to suppress and manipulate the Gedeo people and their wealth. This is a protest song sung by the people to ventilate about their grievances and past agony, and at the same time communicating the community to take revenge on them. Though this is antagonistic, it is a kind of hate speech which bases itself on win-lose situation as expressed in the folk media. Of course, according to Fisher (2000), conflict resolution between ethnic groups takes different forms: win–lose, lose–lose, and win–win. Indeed, the Gedeo apply various ways to resolve their conflicts with other groups. They implement the win–lose approach by condemning their suppressors at a psychological level, as in the above poem, and sometimes through physical violence, though it is usually followed by social cursing done within the social hierarchy. The lose–lose strategy is used to smooth over conflict through compromises reached through the words of the elders. And, there are cases in which they may take the win–win approach so as to maximize the goals of both sides through collaborative problem solving.

The Gedeo do resolve any kind of ethnic conflicts using the *serra* (legal) system. The Gedeo *serra* puts sanctions if conflict breaks out, and urges the parties involved to negotiate. When conflict arises, the *hyiticha*, who are considered as spiritual fathers advise the people to pray. The *gada* father then prays for peace and prosperity among the Gedeo people. The *rogas* and *hyiticha* call for a *songo* to resolve the dispute between the groups. The local elders are sent to the bordering ethnic groups to learn the cause of the conflict, and these messengers communicate with the opposing side. They negotiate and finally come to an agreement.

The Gedeo cherish peaceful coexistence with their neighbouring ethnic groups. The Gedeo spiritual fathers (the *gada*) preach about peace and they try to bring the opponents into agreement.

Conclusion and Recommendations

In Gedeo, the 'traditional' conflict resolution system as folk media has become a good way to make peace and is vital in addressing the social and political issues of the people. This is because it is an indigenous knowledge and communication system, which is transmitted mainly through indigenous communication channels: indigenous organizations, folk media, etc. The Gedeo have a traditional administrative system called the *gada* system. The social fabric of the people is the product of the people's values, beliefs and traditions (Tadesse 2002), which are maintained through folk media. The communication system of the Gedeo works within the tenets of their ancestral wisdom and values. Gedeo's folk media are loaded with the people's philosophy or thoughts; consequently, they demonstrate the values, traditions, norms and belief system that form Gedeo culture. The Gedeo use their folk media to address marriage, boundary, clan and ethnic conflicts. The folk media in Gedeo, perhaps, like elsewhere is part of 'the ritual points of human experience when groups of people must agree on a minimum program of feeling or action' (Wedekind 1977: 2).

The Gedeo, prefer their folk ways or media to modern systems. This is perhaps because they represent the inherent quality of the people's culture and demonstrate the strong bound between the people and their culture. Besides, the desire to keep the indigenous knowledge and communication system intact is highly evident in Gedeo like in other oral societies (Finnegan 2012). And Gedeo's folk media are invaluable in trying to learn and understand the socio-cultural, political and religious thoughts of the people (Finnegan 2012). Since many of the development efforts fail because of a lack of understanding of the societal beliefs, custom, traditional and social thought of a people, it would be advisable to give due attention to the studying of the people's folk media. Thus, studying and preserving folk media is important, not only in order to preserve cultural heritages and the ancestral wisdom of the Gedeo (Asebe 2007), but also to ensure sustainable development and the successful implementation of modern systems. But of course, it requires effort to take into account people's folk media and customary practices alongside modern media and legal systems.

The analysis and discussion made so far on the folk narrations, particularly the folk poems above, indicate that the Gedeo use various ways to resolve conflicts. Gedeo's folk media are vital in addressing psychological and social conflicts. The discourses made through these folk media help smooth over social and family feuds, and help address societal problems since they are the means through which consensus is built, peace is maintained and conflicts are resolved.

References

ABIYOT Legesse, BOGALE Teferi and Axel BAUDOUIN

2013 *Indigenous agroforestry knowledge transmission and young people's participation in agroforestry practices: The case of Wonago Woreda, Gedeo Zone, Southern Ethiopia*. Dilla: Dilla University.

ASEBE Regassa

2007 *Ethnicity and inter-ethnic relations: The 'Ethiopian experiment' and the case of the Guji and Gedeo*. Tromsø: University of Tromsø.

ASMAROM Legesse

1973 *Gada: Three approaches to the study of African society*. New York: The Red Sea Press.

BIRHANE G/Hiwot and MELESSE Maryo

2015 'Evaluation of land use patterns across agro-ecological and slope classes using GIS and remote sensing: The case of Gedeo Zone, southern Ethiopia', *International Journal of Advanced Remote Sensing and GIS* 4(1): 1385–1399.

FINNEGAN, Ruth

2012 *Oral Literature in Africa*. London: Oxford University Press.

FISHER, Caroline J.

2000 'Like it or not ... Culture Matters. Linking Culture to Bottom Line Business Performance'. *Employee Relations Today* 27: 46–49

GETACHEW Senishaw and MAMO Hebo

2015 'Indigenous knowledge system and local ecological management in midland Gedeo: The case of Mekonisa Kebele', in: ASEBE R. Debela et.al. (eds.), *Indigenous peoples rights, indigenous knowledge nexus development*, 35–63. Dilla: Institute of Indigenous Studies, Dilla University.

JOHNSTONE, Barbara

2004 'Discourse analysis and narrative', in: Deborah Shiffrin, Deborah Tannen and Heidi. E. HAMILTON (eds.), *The Handbook of Discourse Analysis*, 635–649. Massachusetts: Blackwell Publishers.

KARLBERG, Michael

2005 'The power of discourse and the discourse of power: Pursuing peace through discourse intervention', *International Journal of Peace Studies* 10(1): 1–23.

KIROS Birhanu, SAMUEL Erkato and DAGNE Shiberu

2014 *Community Situation 2013 Adado, SNNPR.*

LUBO Teferi

2012 'The post 1991 "inter-ethnic" conflicts in Ethiopia: An investigation', *Journal of Law and Conflict Resolution* 4(4): 62–69.

MCQUAIL, Dennis

2000 *McQuail's mass communication theory*. Washington D.C.: SAGE Publications.

MESELE Negash

2007 'Trees management and livelihoods in Gedeo's agroforests, Ethiopia'. *Forests, Trees and Livelihoods* 17(2): 157–168.

NIGUSSIE Meshesha and Kjell Magne YRI

2016 'Socio-political discourse and communication in Sidaama folk media', *Oslo Studies in Languages* 8(1): 339–357.

OISHI, Etsuko

2006 'Austin's speech act theory and the speech situation', *Esercizi Filosofici* 1: 1–14.

SCOLLON, Ron and Suzanne B. K. SCOLLON

1981 *Narrative, literacy, and face in interethnic communication*. Norwood, N.J.: Ablex.

SETEGN, Kifle, BOGALE Teferi, ABARAHAM Kebedom and ABIYOT Legesse

2016 'Factors influencing farmers decisions on the use of introduced soil and water conservation practices in the lowlands of Wenago Woreda, Gedeo Zone, Ethiopia', *American Journal of Rural Development* 4(1): 24–30.

SHMUELI, Deborah F.

(u.d) 'Approaches to conflict resolution', in *Encyclopedia of Life Support Systems* (EOLSS). Retreived on 25/01/2018 from https://www.eolss.net/sample-chapters/C14/E1-40-03.pdf.

TADESSE Beriso

2000 'The riddles of number nine in Guji-Oromo culture', *Journal of Ethiopian Studies* 33(1): 49–66.

TADESSE Jaleta

2004 *A contextual study of Guji Oromo proverbs: Functions in focus*. MA thesis, Addis Ababa University.

TADESSE Kippie

2002 *Five thousand years of sustainability? A case study on Gedeo land use*. PhD Dissertation, Wageningen University.

VALBUENA, Victor T.

1986 *Philippine folk media in development communication*. Singapore: Asian Mass Communication Research and Information Centre.

VANSINA, Jan

1985 *Oral tradition as history*. London: James Currey.

1965 *Oral tradition: A study in historical methodology*. London: Penguin Books.

WEDEKIND, Klaus

1977 *Gedeo work songs in the context of the Ethiopian revolution*. Addis Ababa: SIL International.

YIREFU Tefera, WONDAWEK Abebe and BOGALE Teferi

2016 'Woody plants species diversity of home garden agroforestry in three agroecological zones of Dilla Zuria District, Gedeo Zone, Southern Ethiopia', *International Journal of Fauna and Biological Studies* 3(3): 98–106.

Indigenous Religions, Identity and Biodiversity in Southwest Ethiopia

Lessons from Council of Nationalities-SNNPRS[1] Commissioned Studies

ZERIHUN DODA

Introduction

Existing studies of the peoples of Ethiopia have often been criticized as suffering from methodological and theoretical biases (Mekonen 1990). Historiographical accounts have lacked representations of the full range and diversity of the Ethiopian peoples and cultures (Pankhurst 1990; Bahru 2001), and ethnographic documentations of Southwest Ethiopia have focused on broad surveys of the socio-cultural institutions with few attempts made to synthesize national, interethnic commonalties (Abbink 2000). Studies of the autochthonous religions of Southwest Ethiopia have often been dominated by accounts from diffusionist, evolutionary, and structural functionalist perspectives (Abbink 1998; Freeman 1999). There exists a dearth of studies documenting such religions and their linkages with local biodiversity. Some studies (for example, Stauder 1971) have attempted ecological anthropological analysis of certain ethnic groups in southwest Ethiopia. Although most recent studies (for example, Samuel and Hewlett 2016; Quinlan et al. 2015) have started documenting socio-ecological and ethnobiological systems in the region, studies documenting the interface of native religions and local biodiversity are still lacking.

Empirical studies exploring the mutual interdependence between ecology, biodiversity and traditional religions and their resulting positive effects on society and environment in Ethiopia are scarce. Their coupled existence and endangerment are also little understood. Some emerging studies have generally focused on the role religious places and institutions play in the conservation of biodiversity, such as endangered fauna and flora (Desalegn 2009; Massey et al. 2014). Others have attempted to examine the rel evance of traditional religions and sacred sites from the perspectives of anthropology, politics and jurisprudence (Hamer 2002; Markos et al. 2012; Dillu 2009; Kifle 2014). Studies such as these do not, however, address the socio-ecological and biocultural relevance and values that bind local biodiversity and native religions. In the following, I attempt to report on the coupled existence and endangerment of native religions and local biodiversity from a broadly biocultural diversity perspective, drawing on lessons from studies conducted from 2008–2010 in four Southwest Ethiopian communities, commissioned by the Council of Nationalities (CoNs) and the Christensen Fund (TCF). Data from fieldwork conducted during three trips – in Wonsho Sidama from January to March 2008, in Basketo and Me'enit from June to October 2008, and in Ṭambaro and Sidama from July to September 2009 – is used to provide insights into native-religion-mediated identities, ecology biodiversity and endangerment.

1 Southern Nations, Nationalities and Peoples' Regional State

Methodology

This paper is a collation and synthesis of thematic issues drawn from a set of previous studies on four ethnic groups in Southwest Ethiopia: Sidama, Ṭambaro, Basketo and Me'enit. The paper draws lessons mainly from the studies commissioned by the CoNs-SNNPRS and TCF, in which I participated as a lead researcher. As the main research goal was to document and describe cultural and ethnohistorical phenomena, the study designs varied, and included: collaborative ethnography, documentary analysis; visual documentation; market surveys of ethnohistorical, natural and cultural heritages; and fieldwork involving observations, key informant interviews, group discussions and genealogical studies. There were, in addition, periodic consultative meetings involving feedback and member checks to monitor data and fieldwork quality. Data relevant to the present study thus draws on the wide variety of material that resulted from the project.

Review of Anthropological Works on Southwest Ethiopia

As Abbink (2000) has noted, much of work done in the past on Southwest Ethiopia focused on analysis of the ethnographic present and ethnographic studies of individual ethnic groups, and there are few general analyses of Ethiopian cultures or ethnographic comparisons. The same is true in the area of nature and culture linkages. Anthropological accounts of the native religions of Southwest Ethiopia have often been dominated by accounts from diffusionist and functionalist perspectives (Freeman 1999; Abbink 1998). Explanations of religion and ecology in southwest Ethiopia have pursued a number of approaches. One is the approach that sees religion as a tool that helps local cultures adapt to their particular environments. According to Abbink (2000), ecological conditions are important elements – along with other historical and socio-economic processes – in the formation and transformation of religious identities in southwest Ethiopia.

A related explanation, particularly in regard to the similarities in religions across ethnic groups, also invokes ecological factors. Some authors (for example, Wood 2000) seem to argue that the similarities in religious institutions across different ethnic groups in southwest Ethiopia may be attributed to accidental factors arising from the different peoples inhabiting similar ecological conditions. Ecology is here considered as an explanatory factor, an independent variable that influences the type and nature of religious belief and practice.

Another explanation of the relationship between religion and ecology argues that linkages between ecology and religion in a community may be the result of exchange through inter-ethnic relationships and population movements. So, for example, Freeman (1999) argues that the Gamo highlanders' indigenous forms of religious beliefs and initiation rites may have been adapted from the neighbouring pastoral Oromo and other Cushitic groups: they are the product of population movements and, having once been introduced, they were adapted to their specific ecological conditions.

In summary, approaches employed to study culture, ecology and society in Ethiopia may be classified into four streams: ecological anthropological approaches, which deal with culture, religion and ecology from functional, diffusionist and evolutionary angles; indigenous knowledge and biodiversity conservation approaches, which emphasize the role of indigenous knowledge and religions in natural resource management and conservation of biodiversity; environmental history approaches, which focus on the history of ecological degradation; and emerging socio-ecological approaches, which attempt to trace interactions between ecological and social systems, their mutual sustainability and resilience.

A Better Framework for Understanding Religion, Ecology and Biodiversity?

Biocultural diversity is a concept that signals a connection between biological and cultural diversity (Redford and Brosius 2006). It is "the sum total of the world's differences, no matter what their origin. It includes biological diversity at all its levels, from genes to populations to species to ecosystems; cultural diversity in all its manifestations, ranging from individual ideas to entire cultures; and, importantly, the interactions among all of these" (Harmon and Loh 2005: 231). This approach helps us to see ecological processes not in isolation but in relation to social and cultural processes; it combines both social and ecological systems (Berkes 1999; Berkes et al. 2000). In this context, native religions and local biodiversity, represented – for example – by sacred groves and trees, are resilient social-ecological systems. These systems possess aspects of spatio-temporal constancy and boundedness. However, they are ecologically and socially dynamic and complex, with changing meanings and compositions (Sheridan 2008).

Maffi and Woodley (2010) and Sponsel (2013) provide a useful conceptual framework for this integrative interface between biodiversity and cultural diversity that stresses the inextricable link between the two. The geographical convergence of biological and cultural diversity has, in particular, gained attention. Sponsel calls this the 'diversity principle', while Maffi and Woodley call it the 'true web of life'. The densities of ethnic groups and languages spoken in a given area have been shown to correlate with biocultural diversity richness (Pilgrim et al. 2009) and these are now considered as among key proxy indicators for such diversity.

In summary, the bio-cultural diversity perspective provides a useful framework with which to analyse the interaction, mutual co-adaptation and endangerment of local religions and biodiversity in the context of southwest Ethiopia. The factors that drive the emergence and development of both systems also work towards their coupled endangerment: loss in one means loss in the other.

Key Themes from the Cons and TCF-Commissioned Studies

Religion as identity mediator

Religion is an important identity mediator. With the current fostering of ethnicity in Ethiopia, traditional practices – not the least of which are native religions – are being encouraged, as they are seen as markers of ethnic identity (Freeman 1999). Our findings have shown that local people have started reclaiming their native religious identities. Some aspects of native religions were crucial components of the identities of peoples.

In our studies, people were using their ancestral religions as elements in defining themselves. There was, however, a tendency to lead a double life of allegiance to both ancestral and mainstream religions. Practitioners of ancestral religions were not often vocal about their religious identities, although we met some who were. People were often creative and instrumentalist in their ways of using religion as an identity marker (Mohammed 2012).

In general, as Abbink (2011) notes, religious identities are becoming more dominant as people's primary public identity in Ethiopia.

Religion, ecology, biodiversity and identity

The interactions among religion, ecology and biodiversity are complex, and many dimensions are involved. Among the current diverse perspectives investigating the interface between culture and biodiversity, religion stands out as an important component. Similarly, the biocultural diversity perspective takes religion as an important element in the analysis and understanding of sustainability and the resilience of socio-ecological systems.

More broadly, the interaction between religion and ecology can be further understood in today's current context, in which there is a growing sense of the role world religions play in environmental protection. Religion-motivated, ecologically responsible values, lifestyles and diverse forms of environmentalism are important concerns in the discussion about religion and ecology. With respect to the interaction between religion and biodiversity, important dimensions of the discussion include: the role of religions in promoting environmental and ecological sustainability; and biodiversity conservation and the mutual relationship between various religions and biodiversity. In the current debates about biocultural diversity and endangerment of cultures and biodiversity, religion is a key element: fundamental beliefs and practices attached to a sense of reverence form the basis for morality in behaviour and thinking about ecology and biodiversity. The world's rich biocultural diversity hotspots are more likely to be associated with the presence and practice of deep, pro-ecology and biodiversity friendly moralities and beliefs (Bhagwat et al. 2011).

While the current biocultural diversity literature generally regards the various world religions as having varying degrees of ecological sensitivity and friendliness toward biodiversity, and suggests that – in a sense – all religions in some form shape group identities in relation to ecology (Verschuuren et al. 2010), traditional religions are frequently seen as more ecologically sensitive, that is, much more dependent on, and supportive of, ecologies. In much of the developing world, native religions, local ecologies and biodiversity are intertwined and they form important dimensions in group identities (Sponsel 2012). Ecologically based and biodiversity-dependent religious rituals serve local communities as the locus of maintenance, continuity and expressions of identity (Posey 1999; Sponsel 2016).

Biodiversity and Native Religions in Southwest Ethiopia

Diversities of religion in Southwest Ethiopia

In the studied communities, three categories of religious identities can be broadly recognized: Christianity, Islam and ancestral religions (CSA 2013). Forms of syncretized religious tradition, arising from centuries of transactions between autochthonous and introduced religions, also surface in the religious landscape in Southwest Ethiopia (Braukämper 1992). While these divergent forms may be considered to share some fundamental commonalities, the different religions possess certain unique features. The question of why there is such remarkable diversity, as Abbink (2000) notes, deserves serious comparative ethnological investigation. Consideration of broader historical, socio-economic and ecological conditions is, among other things, important in understanding the nature and peculiarities of religions and their diversities in southwest Ethiopia.

Ecological conditions are key factors both in the historical processes that have contributed to the development of specific religious forms and in the way that the same processes have enabled native religions to adapt to changing ecological and socio-economic conditions. In understanding the group identities of southwest Ethiopia, it is important to consider the role of nature and ecologies.

In our research, certain religious forms were more likely to be practised among different groups. The active interethnic relations that have been ongoing for millennia may be an important historical and socio-economic condition in this process of religious exchange. While religions have, for centuries, been exchanged among peoples, the diverse native regions have also been characterized by shared values in southwest Ethiopia (Abbink 2000). While distinct religions were historically and contemporarily practised among the studied communities, there are discernible similarities among native religions. A first major shared feature is that these religions are nature-based, in that both their belief dimension and practice realm involve the natural world. They are embedded in concrete local ecologies. Biodiversity species become active components: they can be talked to; their natural sights, sounds and other behaviours may be deciphered and consulted for symbolic meanings and messages.

Secondly, belief in the existence of a Supreme Being (*śossa* in Basketo, *magano* in Sidama, *gambala magano* in Ṭambaro and *yeeri-tumma* in Me'enit) who has created everything and in the role of ancestors as mediators is important. This is evidenced throughout Africa, although the concept and identity of the Supreme Being is fairly nebulous. Instead, prayers are addressed to the ancestors who are considered intercessors: the Supreme Being is addressed through the ancestral spirits because most Africans believe that it cannot be addressed directly (Bae 2007).

Thirdly, belief in the power of spirits is important. People believe in both benevolent and malevolent spirit entities: thus, fear, reverence and respect characterize the way believers think, act and do with respect to topographic, ecological and biodiversity dimensions (Cunningham 2001).

A fourth important feature is the fact that certain elements of the biodiversity are important in the manifestation and concretization of religious beliefs and practices. *Podocarpus falcatus*, for example, is an important tree species among Basketo and Sidama; while *macrostacheus croton* and *cordia africana* are important in Ṭambaro and Me'enit. Further, as Freeman (1999) notes, key aspects of ancestral religions such as the concept of divine kings, rain making, initiation and sacrificial rites, and use of ecological resources for religious enactments are also shared elements. This is a result of manifest historical and cultural continuities and exchanges among the various peoples of southwest Ethiopia. It is also evidence of a fundamental connection between culture and nature that manifests itself in fundamentally similar ways in different ecological settings.

Finally, native religions share an important sociological feature – communality. Collective participation in worship events, ritual performances and related ceremonies are important. The preponderance of males as active agents and officiators in these religions, and the manner of socialization and communication of religious symbols, teachings and codes in horizontal and vertical transmission are also important. Knowledge, skills and attitudes are acquired through *in situ* training, learning by doing and experiential engagements.

Religion-Mediated Identity and Biocultural Diversity in Southwest Ethiopia

The southwest Ethiopian communities are important sites of relative abundance of nature-based religions. This has resulted in resilient biocultural diversity mediated by native religions, although mainstream religions – such as Ethiopian Orthodox Christianity – have also been shown to be centres of biocultural diversity (Massey et al. 2014). In Basketo, the *śossa* is a resilient socio-ecological system where there was a co-adaptation between native religion and the cultural keystone tree species – *zigga* (*podocarpus falcatus*), *marra* (*prunus africana*), *wolla* (*ficus vasta*) and *ooch* (*syzygium guineense*), among others. The Sidama sacred forests have served as refuges for over twenty-seven locally and nationally endangered native tree species and scores of fauna, while contributing towards the preservation of local cultural, linguistic and religious diversity and serving as a holistic centre for justice, well-being and peace (Zerihun 2015). Ţambaro traditional religion incorporates the ritual of planting *masincho* (*macrostacheyus croton*) as a symbol of respect and commemoration for paternal ancestors.

As material expressions and representations of religious beliefs, sacred forests and keystone trees are crucial in helping locals to enact and reinforce their religious identities. In a rapidly changing world and in a regional context in which various religions compete for pre-eminence, mainstream religions often supplant ancestral religions (Hamer 2002; Freeman 1999, 2013). The presence of sacred forests and trees imbued with socio-cultural value provides a way for local communities to show the vitality of their ancestral religious identity (Maffi and Woodley 2010).

Sacred forests and individual woody trees are 'mirror images' of the local community: their identity embodies their past, present and future (Fincke and Oviedo 2008; Nazarea 1998; Rival 1998). Sacred trees are likened to ancestors, embodying the custodian community's sense of identity and concretizing their spatial-temporal existence. Through them, the community meets its deepest theological quests, reaffirms its identity, reinforces its values, commemorates its ancestors, and placates its deities (Dafni 2007; Toledo 2013). The identity-conferring role of native religions working through the mediation of ecology and biodiversity has now been officially recognized in the Millennium Ecosystem Assessment as an example of a cultural ecosystem service (De Groot et al. 2005).

Endangerment and Loss of Native Religions

A major observation from our studies in all communities was the precarious state of native religions. Much worse, many religions were already dead. It is generally agreed that ethnocide – the death of cultures – has occurred across the world. Language endangerment has also been fairly well documented and, in the following, I explore how existing models of language endangerment may be adapted to the case of religion. But first, below is a review of local explanations of endangerment.

Local peoples' explanatory models may capture the realities of the endangerment and loss of their religions in tangible ways. The idea of a generational gap in the practise of native religions provides one model, and is expressed by comments from interlocutors such as: 'the present generation no longer respects ancestral traditions', 'this generation knows nothing about ancestral values' and 'young people go and cut sacred trees because they no more are afraid of retributions of ancestors'. Other comments relating to generational gap reveal a perception that the practice of native religions is an old person's profession. There is talk about the number of practitioners and the fact that very few people now adhere to the native religions, indicated in comments such as: 'you can count them in your fingers', 'there are very few households who practise it'. The marginalization status model explains endangerment in relation to spatial location. People would often talk about how native religions are now relegated to obscure corners in inaccessible, remote areas. Among the Me'enit, for example, the practising of native religions was reported as being limited to peripheral areas.

The clandestine ways in which some native religions are conducted provides another explanatory model. Thus, local people often talked about individuals 'conducting the religion in hiding', 'in the dark secret places', or in the 'late night hours'. The very low social status accorded to some native religions may, thus, indicate their endangerment. Among the Ţambaro, for example, practising Fandano[2] was considered as a *shufuro* – a contemptible thing that some deviant people practice in hiding.

Finally, there is also an explanatory model relating to time. People would often talk about native religions being practised in the past, indicating that they were no longer active – a fact that could be confirmed by observations of sacred groves that are now the sites of markets, schools or government offices. They would often talk about the time when localities were teeming with sacred groves and spirit possession cults. In some cases, local models also relate the virtual death of the religion, when they make explicit mention of the confirmatory statement: 'Now, this is no more practised in this community'.

Adapting Models of Language Endangerment

Literature on biocultural diversity has a good starting point in the models developed by UNESCO (2003) and Ethnologue (Simons and Lewis 2013), which use factors such as the number and age of active speakers, the documented status of the language, and whether it is used in official contexts or limited to home use, among others, to measure the endangerment status of a language.

The metaphor of the death of languages is well known in explanations of the endangerment and loss of native languages across the world. What Dessalegn (2013) notes about the endangerment status and 'death' of certain native languages in southwest Ethiopia may well be applicable to many native religions in Ethiopia. Whether it is a language or a religion that is exposed to the process of dying, the wealth of inherited knowledge disappears with the passing away of the last active practitioner.

2 An ancient syncretic religion forged out of the admixture of native beliefs and Islamic faith that used to be common among the Hadiya, Marakqo, Tambaro, Kambata and other neighbouring ethnic groups but is now moribund.

What makes the case of religious endangerment unique when compared to that of language is the fact that religious ideologies and practices tend to be, in the context of native cultures, more dependent on the ecological and biodiversity components of the locality in which they occur. The death of a religion not only exposes the associated ecological, socio-economic and cultural factors to danger, it also entails the death of certain dimensions of local language that are unique to the religion.

One of the commonly employed models for measuring language endangerment uses five points on a scale that focuses on the chances of intergenerational transmission and the extent and profile of current users of the language: potentially endangered, endangered, seriously endangered, terminally endangered and dead (Wurm 2001). A language is potentially endangered if the users are children and they prefer speaking the dominant language; it is terminally endangered or moribund if the only speakers are a few old, dying people; and it is practically dead when the last speaker dies. This scale of measurement may be adapted to religions. Many religions have died in southwest Ethiopia with the death of the last effective practitioners, or with shifts to other religions. In the studies we have undertaken, many native religions may be said to be already dead; and the few in existence were practised by very old people. Terminally endangered or moribund would be a good way to describe those religions that do exist. However, it should be noted that there may be intra-regional and intra-community variations in the endangerment level of these religions.

Endangerment and Loss of Native Religions: Main Drivers

In all the studied communities, the main drivers of endangerment among native religions were government policies, modernization, urbanization, demographic pressure leading to outmigration and the limiting of access to biodiversity and ecological resources that were previously reserved for religious purposes, and – most importantly – conversion to modern religions, especially Protestant Christianity (Freeman 2013; Awoke 2016; Zerihun 2015). Traditional religion has suffered big losses since the 1950s, coinciding with the introduction and expansion of modern religions, which encourage native converts to distance themselves from ancestral rituals (Hamer 1970, 2002; Awoke 2016).

The endangerment of local religions in southwest Ethiopia was often evidenced by the associated decline and endangerment of local biodiversity. Observations and testimonies from our studied communities attest to this condition. Existing places of biocultural diversity in Sidama, Ṭambaro, Me'enit and Basketo were invariably associated with the remnants of resilient native religions. The degraded states of existing sacred groves, continuing socio-economic, demographic, modernizing and religious transformation and development policy continue to endanger native religions and the local biodiversity they depend on.

Globally, evidence is mounting of an increasing loss of the rich diversity in nature and culture (Smith and Maffi 2001; Sponsel 2013). Among the notable dimensions of this loss is in linguistic diversity (Mishler and Maffi 2001; Zent and Maffi 2001; Loh and Harmon 2014), which Mühlhäusler (2001) refers to as 'eco-linguistic diversity losses'. Ethnobotanical and forest-related knowledge loss is another key aspect (Ford 2001; Shiva 1998; Snape 1996). Traditional religions in African and other small-scale societies are increasingly threatened with extinction and replacement by modern value systems (Gellar 2007). The loss of indigenous crops, trees and endemic animal species in many parts of the world is linked to the loss of religions and traditional knowledge systems related to these species.

Syncretism and the Future of Native Religions

The term 'syncretism' denotes the coalescence of cultural traits in its broadest sense, but is often employed with reference to religion (Braukämper 1992). Syncretism in religion is an important phenomenon in Ethiopia. As a religiously diverse country, with two major world religions present from its beginning, there has been the opportunity for syncretism driven by multiple factors in Ethiopia. Among the communities studied, aspects of native religions and identities existed in syncretic ways, although native religions were often shrouded under the cloak of mainstream religions (Mohammed 2012).

While the linked endangerment of religions and biodiversity was evident in southwest Ethiopia, the socio-ecological system of native religions and local biodiversity was, nonetheless, resilient. A strategy of adopting an accommodative approach to other religions seems to have been employed and a number of native religions have acquired a pidgin nature in which dominant elements from mainstream and ancestral religions have combined to form a new entity (Braukämper 1992).

In spite of the fact that most native religions are seriously endangered, recent attempts at reviving them seem to be helping secure the continuance of at least some of these religions, including the Sidama ancestral religion, the *śossa* in Basketo and the *gambala magano* religion in Ṭambaro. Syncretism may, thus, be an important factor in the continuity of at least certain elements of traditional religions in the region.

Significance, Implications and Future Directions

These studies may be considered as preliminary attempts at a biocultural perspective on religion, ecology and biodiversity in southwest Ethiopia. The studies contribute to mapping endangered and lost native religions in the region from a systematic perspective. Further, the attempt to document the endangerment of native religions has revealed a link with similar endangerment to local biodiversity, and the demonstration that existing biocultural hotspots in the region are largely mediated by the maintenance of traditional religions is an important contribution to the current debates on culture, environment, conservation and development. The studies have documented religion-mediated biocultural diversity hotspots, bringing these to the attention of concerned stakeholders, including policy makers, local communities and researchers.

Summary and Conclusion

The CoNs and TCF in partnership with regional universities have been engaged in this process of documentation since the late 2000s. CoNs is currently continuing these studies with a focus on documenting shared values among the various ethnic groups in the region. In the last ten years, dozens of research outputs have been produced. But a synthesis of these works and the core lessons they contain is currently lacking, and is essential in order to reflect on the relevance, contributions and limitations of these studies. The present paper was conceived with this in mind and driven by a keen interest in the themes of native religion, ecology and biodiversity and their linked endangerment, with the aim of evaluating how a subset of the CoNs and TCF commissioned studies addressed these themes.

The paper has shown the CoN and TCF commissioned studies have contributed towards a preliminary mapping of native religions, their role as identity markers, their mediation in ecological sustainability and biocultural diversity, and their endangerment owing to a range of drivers.

From the foregoing discussion, it can be concluded that:

- Diverse, yet fundamentally related, native religions sharing some salient features have existed, and continue to exist, in southwest Ethiopia.
- The native religions of southwest Ethiopia are fundamentally nature-based and underpinned by ecological sensitivity and support for biodiversity, but they are also dependent on biodiversity for their resilience.
- Native religions have been and are important mediators of group identity in southwest Ethiopia, and the uniqueness of such identities lies in their basic attachment to ecology and biodiversity.
- While native religions in southwest Ethiopia have been dynamic and resilient, a range of factors have driven these to a precarious state of existence, endangering both the religions and the biodiversity they support and depend on.
- Thus, while many native religions are either moribund or already dead, some continue to exist and an important variable in their future existence appears to be creative syncretism, which – while it potentially introduces basic changes to the original constitution of the autochthonous religion – may positively contribute to its continuity.

Implications and Future Directions

To further our current understanding of sustainable societies, cultures and ecologies, it is imperative that we should be concerned with those native religions that have been shown to have positive ecological values, while acknowledging that native religions do not necessarily contribute towards positive socio-ecological systems (Cunningham 2001). Documenting and protecting native religions in southwest Ethiopia is a matter of preserving useful cultural diversity and of protecting basic human rights enshrined in the country's constitution and in related international conventions. It is further justified by the pragmatic utility of native religions as instruments of socio-cultural wellbeing, jurisprudence, peace-making and conflict resolution; and by the conservational values of such religions, in as much as they promote biodiversity.

At the global scale, arguments for preserving native religions as core elements in biocultural diversity rest on a set of values that includes the link between the biological and cultural diversity and the positive role of traditional religions in conservation (Pilgrim and Pretty 2010; Loh and Harmon 2014; International Society of Ethnobiology n.d.). Addressing the loss of both through a holistic approach is global society's urgent assignment and its 'ethno-ecological' (Zent et al. 1999) and 'moral-ethical' (Harmon 2001) imperative. As a matter of basic human rights, cultural survival and compensation for past colonial crimes (Posey and Dutfield 1996), we must strive to understand and secure the richness of ethno-ecological knowledge in areas of rich biodiversity (Maffi 2001; Harmon 2001); the conservation knowledge in endangered languages and religions (Maffi 2001); the role of religion in ecology and the convergence of biocultural diversity hotspots in native religious areas (Bhagwat et al. 2011); and the practical development and livelihood benefits of preserving these heritages.

The implications and future directions arising from the foregoing discussions and conclusion include the following:

- Further mixed methods research needs to be undertaken to systematically document and map the linked endangerment of religions and biodiversity in southwest Ethiopia and beyond.
- Systematic measurement tools for determining the endangerment scales of the religions of the region and the country at large need to be produced.
- Religion-mediated bioculturally diverse hotspots in the region and the country at large need to be comprehensively surveyed and documented.
- The role of native religions in the formation, expression and maintenance of group identities and how these depend on local ecologies and biodiversity need further and large-scale systematic study.
- Biocultural hotspots need further systematic documentation using visual anthropological methodologies.
- Actionable projects aimed at revitalizing biodiversity-friendly, moribund and highly endangered religions and working towards mitigating existing drivers of endangerment need to be developed.

Acknowledgements

I want to thank Hawassa University, Ethiopia and the Frankfurt Frobenius Institute, Germany, for providing us with the chance to be part of the international conference that took place in February 2017 at Hawassa City, Ethiopia, and for facilitating publication of our papers in this journal. Further, I also want to thank the Council of Nationalities, SNNPRS and TCF for commissioning and funding the studies on peoples and cultures of southwest Ethiopia, on which I was invited to take the role of a lead researcher.

References

ABBINK, Jon

1998 'An historical-anthropological approach to Islam in Ethiopia: Issues of identity and politics'. *Journal of African Cultural Studies* 11(2): 109–124.

2000 'Comparing cultures in Ethiopia: From ethnography to generative explanations'. *Northern African Studies* 7(3): 1–14.

2011 'Religion in public spaces: Emerging Muslim-Christian polemics in Ethiopia'. *African Affairs* 110(439): 253–274.

AWOKE Amzaye Assoma

2016 'Religious change among the Kore: Politics and Christianity in Southwestern Ethiopia'. *Sociology and Anthropology* 4(1): 29–36.

BAE, Chom Sup

2007 *Ancestor worship and the challenges it poses to the Christian mission and ministry.* PhD Dissertation, Faculty of Theology, University of Pretoria.

BAHRU Zewde

2001 *A history of modern Ethiopia, 1855–1991* (Second Edition). Oxford: James Currey; Athens: Ohio University Press.

BERKES, Fikret

1999 *Sacred ecology: Traditional ecological knowledge and resource management.* Philadelphia: Taylor & Francis.

BERKES, Fikret, Johan COLDING and Carl FOLKE

2000 'Rediscovery of traditional ecological knowledge as adaptive management'. *Ecological Applications* 10(5): 1251–1262.

BHAGWAT, Shonil A., Nigel DUDLEY and Stuart R. HARROP

2011 'Religious following in biodiversity hotspots: Challenges and opportunities for conservation and development'. *Conservation Letters* 4(3): 234–240.

BRAUKÄMPER, Ulrich

1992 'Aspects of religious syncretism in Southern Ethiopia'. *Journal of Religion in Africa* 22(3): 194.

CENTRAL STATISTICAL AGENCY (CSA)

2013 *Population projection of Ethiopia for all regions at Wereda level from 2014–2017.* Federal Democratic Republic of Ethiopia.

CUNNINGHAM, Anthony

2001 *Applied ethnobotany: People, wild plant use and conservation.* London: Routledge.

DAFNI, Amots

2007 'Rituals, ceremonies and customs related to sacred trees with a special reference to the Middle East'. *Journal of Ethnobiology and Ethnomedicine* 3: 28.

DE GROOT, Rudolf et al.

2005 'Cultural and amenity services', in: Rashid Hassan, Robert Scholes, Neville Ash (eds.), *Ecosystems and human well-being: Current state and trends. Findings of the condition and trends, volume 1*, 455–476. Washington, D.C.: Island Press.

DESALEGN Desissa

2009 'Indigenous sacred sites and biocultural diversity: A case study from Southwestern Ethiopia'. http://www.terralingua.org/bcdconservation/?p=62, accessed 21 June, 2017.

DESSALEGN Gebeyehu

2013 'On the verge of dying: Languages in Ethiopia', OGMIOS Newsletter 5, 3–6.

DILLU Shaleka

2009 'A study of a local religious institution among the Sidama of Southern Ethiopia'. http://www.humanosphere.cseas.kyoto-u.ac.jp/images/library/Image/report/2009_fs_dilu_e.pdf, accessed 15 June, 2017.

FINCKE, Annelie and Gonzalo OVIEDO

2008 'Bio-cultural diversity and indigenous peoples journey. Report from the 4th IUCN World Conservation Congress Forum, 6–9 October 2008, Barcelona, Spain'. https://cmsdata.iucn.org/downloads/bcd_ip_report_low_res.pdf, accessed 6 June 2018.

FORD, Richard

2001 'Introduction: Ethnobiology at the crossroads'. In: Richard I. Ford (ed.), *Ethnobotany at the millennium: Past promise and future prospects*. Ann Arbor: Museum of Anthropology, University of Michigan.

FREEMAN, Dena Gail

1999 *Transforming traditions: The dynamics of cultural variation in the Gamo Highlands, Southwest Ethiopia*. PhD thesis, London School of Economics, University of London.

2013 'Pentecostalism in a rural context: Dynamics of religion and development in Southwest Ethiopia'. *PentecoStudies* 2(12): 231–249.

GELLAR, Sheldon

2007 'Varieties of religious doctrines and institutions in Africa and their impact on democratization processes', paper presented at the *International Conference on Religious Ideas and Institutions and Transitions to Democracy in Africa, May 18-19, 2007*. http://dlc.dlib.indiana.edu/dlc/handle/10535/4171, last accessed 15 May 2017.

HAMER, John

1970 'Sidāma generational class cycles. A political gerontocracy', *Africa* 40: 50–70.

2002 'The religious conversion process among the Sidāma of North-East Africa', *Africa* 72(4): 598–627.

HARMON, David

2001 'On the meaning and moral of imperative of diversity', in: Luisa Maffi (ed.), *On biocultural diversity: Linking language, knowledge, and the environment*, 53–70. Washington: Smithsonian Institution Press.

HARMON, David and Jonathan LOH

2005 'A global index of biocultural diversity', *Ecological Indicators* 5(3): 231–241.

INTERNATIONAL SOCIETY OF ETHNOBIOLOGY

N.d. 'Declaration of Belem'. http://ethnobiology.net/global-coalition/declaration-of-belem/, accessed 15 June, 2017.

KIFLE Wansamo

2014 'Introduction to Sidama religion'. http://www.afrikaworld.net/afrel/sidama.htm, accessed 22 May 2017.

LOH, Jonathan and David HARMON

2014 *Biocultural diversity: Threatened species, endangered languages*. WWF Netherlands.

MAFFI, Luisa (ed.)

2001 *On biocultural diversity linking language, knowledge and the environment*. Washington D.C.: Smithsonian Institution Press.

MAFFI, Luisa and Ellen WOODLEY

2010 *Biocultural diversity conservation: A global sourcebook*. London, Washington D.C.: Earthscan.

MARKOS Tekile et.al.

2012 *The history and culture of the Sidama nation*. Addis Ababa: Sidama Zone Culture, Tourism & Government Communication Affairs Department, Hawassa. (In Amharic).

MASSEY, Ashley, Shonil BHAGWAT and Kathy MINNIS

2014 'Religious Forest Sites'. http://www.biodiversity.ox.ac.uk/researchthemes/biodiversity-beyond-protected-areas/religious-forest-sites/, accessed 24 September 2014.

MEKONEN Bishaw

1990 'Current status and future directions of socio-cultural studies in Ethiopia', in: Richard Pankhurst and Taddese Beyenne (eds.), *Proceedings of the symposium of Silver Jubilee Anniversary of the lES*, 105–119. Addis Ababa: Addis Ababa University Press.

MISHLER, Brent and Luisa MAFFI, Eds.

2001 'Biodiversity and the loss of lineages', in: Luisa Maffi (ed.), *On biocultural diversity linking language, knowledge and the environment*, 71–81. Washington and London: The Smithsonian Institution.

MOHAMMED Girma

2012 *Understanding religion and social change in Ethiopia*. New York: Palgrave Macmillan.

MÜHLHÄUSLER, Peter

2001 'Eco-linguistics, linguistic diversity, ecological diversity', in: Luisa Maffi (ed.), *On biocultural diversity linking language, knowledge and the environment*, 113–145. Washington and London: The Smithsonian Institution.

NAZAREA, Virginia

1998 *Cultural memory and biodiversity*. Tucson: University of Arizona Press.

PANKHURST, Richard

1990 'Some notes in foreign historiography on Ethiopia', in: Richard Pankhurst and Taddese Beyenne (eds.), *Proceedings of the symposium of Silver Jubilee Anniversary of the IES*. Addis Ababa: Addis Ababa University Press.

PILGRIM, Sarah, Jules PRETTY, Bill ADAMS et al.

2009 'The intersections of biological diversity and cultural diversity: Towards integration', *Conservation and Society* 7(2): 100–112.

PILGRIM, Sarah, and Jules PRETTY

2010 *Nature and culture: Rebuilding lost connections*. London: Earthscan.

POSEY, Darrell Addison

1999 'Introduction: Culture and nature – the inextricable link', in: Darrel Addison Posey (ed.), *Cultural and spiritual values of biodiversity*, 3–18. Nairobi: United Nations Environment Program.

POSEY, Darrell Addison and Graham DUTFIELD

1996 *Beyond intellectual property: Toward traditional resource rights for indigenous peoples and local communities*. Ottawa: International Development Research Centre.

QUINLAN, Robert J. et.al.

2015 'Vulnerability and resilience of Sidama enset and maize darms in Southwestern Ethiopia', *Journal of Ethnobiology* 35(2): 314–336.

REDFORD, Kent and Peter BROSIUS

2006 'Diversity and homogenization in the endgame', *Global Environmental Change* 16(4): 317–319

RIVAL, Laura

1998 *The social life of tees: Anthropological perspectives on tree symbolism*. Oxford, New York: Berg.

SAMUEL Jilo Dira and Barry S. HEWLETT

2016 'Learning to survive ecological risks among Sidama of Southwestern Ethiopia', *Journal of Ecological Anthropology* 18(1): 7.

SHERIDAN, Michael

2008 'The dynamics of African sacred groves: ecological, social and symbolic processes', in: Michael J. Sheridan and Celia Nyamweru (ed.), *African sacred groves: Ecological dynamics and social change*, 9–41. London: James Currey.

SHIVA, Vandana

1998 *Biopiracy: The plunder of nature and knowledge*. London: The Gaya Foundation.

SIMONS, Gary and Paul LEWIS

2013 The World's Languages in Crisis: A 20-Year Update. In Language Death, Endangerment, Documentation, and Revitalization. Wisconsin, Milwaukee. http://www-01.sil.org/~simonsg/preprint/Wisconsin%20Symposium.pdf, accessed February 7, 2017.

SMITH, Eric and Luisa MAFFI (eds.)

2001 'On the co-evolution of cultural, linguistic and biological diversity', in: Luisa Maffi (ed.), *On biocultural diversity linking language, knowledge and the environment*, 95–118. Washington and London: The Smithsonian Institution.

SNAPE, William

1996 *Biodiversity and the law*. Washington DC: Island Press.

SPONSEL, Leslie E.

2012 *Spiritual ecology: A quiet revolution*. Santa Barbara: Praeger Publishers Inc.

2013 'Human impact on biodiversity, overview', in: Simon A. Levin (ed.), *Encyclopedia of biodiversity* (Second Edition), 137–152. Waltham: Academic Press.

2016 *Spiritual ecology, sacred places, and biodiversity conservation*. Routledge Handbooks Online. https://www.routledgehandbooks.com/doi/10.4324/9781315768946.ch11, accessed 18 June 2017.

STAUDER, Jack

1971 *The Majangir: Ecology and society of a Southwest Ethiopian people*. Cambridge: Cambridge University Press.

TOLEDO, Víctor Manuel

2013 'Community conservation and ethnoecology: The three dimensions of local-level biodiversity maintenance', in: Luciana Porter-Bolland et.al. (eds.), *Community action for conservation*, 13–24. New York: Springer.

UNESCO Ad Hoc Expert Group on Endangered Languages

2003 *Language vitality and endangerment*. UNESCO. http://www.unesco.org/culture/ich/doc/src/00120-EN.pdf, accessed 7 February 2017.

VERSCHUUREN, Bas, Robert WILD, Jeffrey MCNEELY and Gonzalo OVIEDO (eds.)

2010 *Sacred natural sites: Conserving nature and culture*. London, Washington D.C: Routledge.

WOOD, John

2000 'The similarities of difference: Symbolic reversals among East Africa's Gabra and their neighbors', *Northeast African Studies* 7(3): 59–84.

WURM Stephen (ed.).

2001 *Atlas of the world's languages in danger of disappearing* (Second Edition). Paris: UNESCO Publishing/Pacific Linguistics.

ZENT, Stanford, Ted L. GRAGSON, and Ben G. BLOUNT

1999 'The quandary of conserving ethnoecological knowledge: A Piaroa example', in: Ted L. Gragson and Ben G. Blount (eds.), *Ethnoecology, Knowledge, Resources and Rights*, 90-124. Athens, Georgia: The University of Georgia Press.

ZENT, Stanford and Luisa MAFFI

2001 'Acculturation and ethnobiological knowledge loss among the Piaroa of Venezuela: Demonstration of a quantitative method for the empirical study of traditional ecological knowledge change', in: Luisa Maffi (ed.), *On biocultural diversity linking language, knowledge and the environment*, 190–212. Washington and London: The Smithsonian Institution.

ZERIHUN Doda Doffana

2015 "*Dagucho (podocarpus falcatus) is abbo!*" *Wonsho sacred sites, Sidama, Ethiopia: Origins, maintenance motives, consequences and conservation threats*. PhD Thesis, University of Kent. http://oatd.org/oatd/record?record=oai%5C%3Aethos.bl.uk%5C%3A646935, accessed 5 June 2017.

List of Contributors

Bosha Bombe has earned a BA in History and an MA in Social Anthropology from Bahir Dar University and Addis Ababa University, respectively. He did intensive fieldwork among the Ganta people in the Gamo Highlands and the Alle people in southwestern Ethiopia. Between March 2014 and September 2016 he was employed as a research associate at Arba Minch University, and since September 2016 he has worked as a lecturer in the Department of Sociology and Social Anthropology at the same university. His research interests focus on: social institutions, social exclusion and integration, slave heritage, identity and poltics, kinship, marriage and family, ethnic identity, boundaries and citizenship, children issues, culture and gender.

Elias Alemu obtained a PhD in Social Anthropology from the University of Bergen and is currently Assistant Professor of Social Anthropology in the College of Social Sciences and Humanities at Hawassa University, serving as coordinator of the MA programme. Over the past fifteen years he has been engaged in teaching in various Higher Education Institutions and researching themes including: masculinity/femininity, violence, gender-based violence, workplace harassment, ethnogenesis, development intervention and local reaction, tourism, intangible cultural heritage, and migration in Ethiopia. Outside Hawassa University, he collaborates with different international and local NGOs as a consultant on qualitative data collection techniques.

Susanne Epple earned her MA and PhD degrees in Social Anthropology from Mainz University. She has done extensive fieldwork on age and gender relations in southern Ethiopia, working among the Bashada since 1994 and the Bayso since 2012. From 2007 to 2015 she was Assistant Professor at the Department of Social Anthropology, Addis Ababa University in Ethiopia. Since 2015, she has been based at the Frobenius Institute in Frankfurt, Germany, and since 2016 she has been a research affiliate at Arba Minch University, Ethiopia. She is currently working on marginalized groups and legal pluralism in southern Ethiopia. Her interests lie in the areas of gender and age in pastoral societies, social discourse and identity, hereditary status groups, cultural and legal pluralism, and human rights.

Getachew Senishaw is Assistant Professor of Social Anthropology at Addis Ababa University. He earned his PhD in Social Anthropology from Addis Ababa University, for which he conducted extensive fieldwork in Gedeo, southern Ethiopia. Before becoming an assistant professor in 2015, he worked at the Authority for Research and Conservation of Cultural Heritage as a senior researcher and director in various departments. In addition, he has undertaken various consultancy works on cultural and social issues for organizations that include UNESCO. He has published several articles and book chapters and his current fields of interest are: indigenous knowledge, environment, livelihoods and heritage management.

Hanna Getachew is Assistant Professor of Social Anthropology, currently serving as Dean of the School of Graduate Studies, at Hawassa University. She obtained a BA in Sociology and Social Administration and an MA in Social Anthropology in 2001 and 2007 from Addis Ababa University, having previously received a PhD in Anthropology and Linguistic-Historical Studies from the University of Messina in 2014. Over the past fifteen years, Hanna has gathered an enormous amount of experience in both research and teaching through working at the South Omo Research Center and Hawassa University. Her research interests include: tourism, marriage and family, indigenous knowledge systems, formal education, museum and public education, heritage management and globalization.

Kansite Gellebo earned an MA in Social Anthropology from Addis Ababa University after gaining a B.Ed in History from Mekelle University. Currently, he is Chairman of the Sociology and Social Anthropology Department at Arba Minch University. His main research interests include: Konso culture, social change, social marginalization, material culture and public places.

Nigussie Meshesha is currently Associate Professor of Journalism and Mass Communication in the School of Journalism and Communication, Addis Ababa University. He completed his PhD in Journalism and Mass Communication, specializing in political and development communication, at Andhra University India, after completing an MA in Public Administration and a Postgraduate Diploma in Theater Direction at the same university. He also obtained an MA in English Literature and BA in Foreign Languages and Literature from Addis Ababa University, and studied Law at Hawassa University. Dr. Nigussie was the Dean of the College of Social Sciences & Humanities, Hawassa University from 2011 to 2017, and also served as the head of a department and coordinator of the postgraduate programme for Journalism and Mass communication for more than a year (2016–2017). He has been a journalist and an educator, and has conducted research in the areas of culture, media and communication, and politics.

Sophia Thubauville is a research fellow and Head of Library at the Frobenius Institute, Frankfurt am Main. She earned a PhD from Mainz University, for which she conducted extensive field research on gender issues among the Maale of southern Ethiopia. Currently, she is involved in a research project on Ethiopia's university boom and the migration of Indian lecturers to the country, as well as in a project to digitize and publish an online database of the archival material on Ethiopian Studies at the Frobenius Institute. Her current fields of interest are: gender, higher education and migration.

Temechegn Gutu received an MA in Social Anthropology from Addis Ababa University and a BA in History from Jimma University. He has been a lecturer in Social Anthropology at Arba Minch University since 2010, and Director of South Omo Research Center (SORC) since 2017. He has done intensive fieldwork among the Alle community and in the Gamo highlands. His research interests lie in: the anthropology of politics, legal anthropology, development anthropology, polygamy, indigenous knowledge and livelihood. He is currently part of a team researching the shared values of Omotic people in the former North Omo Zone, a project sponsored by the Council of Nationalities of the SNNPR.

Zerihun Doda is currently Assistant Professor of Social Anthropology and Sociology at the College of Social Sciences and Humanities, Hawassa University. He has a PhD in Anthropology and Bio-cultural Diversity Management and Conservation from the School of Anthropology and Conservation at the University of Kent, and a MA in Social Anthropology from Addis Ababa University. His research experience and interests lie in ethnographic survey and ethnohistorical research, identity, livelihoods, the nature–culture nexus, ethnobiology, traditional conservation, health and economic development and their socio-cultural impacts.